LIFE OF THE TRAIL 4 HISTORIC HIKES IN
EASTERN JASPER NATIONAL PARK

LIFE OF THE TRAIL 4 HISTORIC HIKES IN
EASTERN JASPER NATIONAL PARK

By Emerson Sanford & Janice Sanford Beck

Rocky
Mountain Books
VANCOUVER • VICTORIA • CALGARY

Rocky Mountain Books   Rocky Mountain Books
#108 – 17665 66A Avenue   PO Box 468
Surrey, BC V3S 2A7   Custer, WA
www.rmbooks.com   98240-0468

Library and Archives Canada Cataloguing in Publication

Sanford, Emerson
    Historic hikes in eastern Jasper National Park / by Emerson Sanford & Janice Sanford Beck.

(Life of the trail 4)
Includes bibliographical references and index.

ISBN 978-1-897522-42-4

    1. Hiking—Alberta—Jasper National Park—Guidebooks.
2. Trails—Alberta—Jasper National Park—Guidebooks.
3. Hiking—Alberta—Jasper National Park—History. 4. Jasper National Park (Alta.)—Guidebooks. 5. Mountaineers—Alberta—Jasper National Park—Biography. I. Sanford Beck, Janice, 1975- II. Title. III. Series.

GV199.44.C22A4584 2009   796.51097123'32   C2008-907157-3

Front cover photo by Emerson Sanford
Back cover photo courtesy of the Whyte Museum of the Canadian Rockies (V14 ACOP-369)
All interior images supplied by the authors except as otherwise noted

Printed in Canada

Rocky Mountain Books acknowledges the financial support for its publishing program from the Government of Canada through the Book Publishing Industry Development Program (BPIDP), Canada Council for the Arts, and the province of British Columbia through the British Columbia Arts Council and the Book Publishing Tax Credit.

Gravel sifts through his worn treads
rhythmically rambling
over roots, rocks and stumps
through raging rivers, up snowy mountain peaks.

Sun soaks his drawn coat
Drenching his brow with sweat
the smell of warm pine, seeping sap
brings curl to his wind chapped lips.

As he clambers up steep mountain passes
Insurmountable beauty spreads before him
the creatures of the forest
remove their cloaks of trees and shrubs.

Night is falling.
He slips into his nylon home
drifting off to bubbling water, zippers zipping
the howl of hidden wolves.

He dreams of unseen sights
where tomorrow's feet might take him.
Tired and sore, they will not slow
faltering only at the firm, false feel of asphalt.

–Susan Sanford Blades, written for her dad, 2006.

Contents

INTRODUCTION

Even as the number of roads, hotels, restaurants and visitor attractions in the Canadian Rockies increase, the peaks and valleys tenaciously maintain their mystical charm. For millennia, people have been walking or riding along whatever trails they could find or create, making their way through the insurmountable beauty – and sometimes insurmountable challenges – of the mountains, surrounded by the sounds of the creatures of the forest.

This volume will transport you through four periods of exploration in the eastern portion of today's Jasper National Park. The first period of exploration was that of Aboriginal use, primarily for the purposes of trade and hunting. When the Colemans first travelled along the Brazeau River, they were greeted by tepee poles stacked against a cliff, old sheep skulls and fire pits. James McEvoy also found Native artifacts along the South Boundary Trail in 1898, leading to him to conclude that Jacques Cardinal had followed an old Native trail in the 1820s.

Trade was also the key motivating factor during the second period of exploration, that of the fur trade. In the early nineteenth century, European traders engaged Aboriginal guides to lead them through their territory to the lucrative fur-trading districts of the West. The journals many of these traders kept for their employers allow us a glimpse into life on the trail during this period.

By 1858, when the British government commissioned Captain John Palliser to explore the Canadian West, trade needs were being superseded by the interests of colonization. The third period of exploration, that of the scientists and railway men, centred on determining the agricultural, mineral and transportation potential of the West, in hopes of encouraging settlement that would strengthen Britain's (and later Canada's) claim on the western provinces.

The 1885 completion of the Canadian Pacific Railway through the southern Rockies ushered in a new era of exploration: that of the tourist-explorers and mountaineers. These easterners, keen to experience new vistas, scale unknown peaks and capture the magnificent game of the Rockies, played an enormous role in establishing the system of alpine trails we know today.

More accurately, however, it was their guides and outfitters who ought to be credited with the tough work required to establish these trails. With Egyptian cotton and nylon tents and asphalt yet to come, early adventure tourism in the Rockies would not have been possible without the use of pack horses – most often led by professional guides and outfitters. These men's efforts to lead their clients to the peaks and valleys of their dreams substantially increased the number of identifiable trails through the Rockies.

The establishment of Canada's system of national parks was another important factor in building today's network of trails. In 1885 the Banff Hot Springs Reserve was established: two years later, it was expanded into Rocky Mountains Park (today's Banff National Park). Today's Jasper National Park was first protected in 1907. With the 1909 introduction of Fire and Game Guardians in Rocky Mountains Park, rapid travel through the mountains became increasingly important, and a network of trails was introduced to simplify the guardians' work enforcing park regulations. By 1914 the guardian service was patrolling some 60 trails though the park. By 1920 the new Warden Service was patrolling 1,400 miles (2253 kilometres) of trails. The side explorations these wardens engaged in during their patrols are responsible for at least some of the non-historic trails through the parks.

The fourth period of exploration winds up just before the period of modern tents and asphalt, a time when road construction and the development of lightweight camping equipment was eliminating the need for the horses and guides of earlier periods. By the mid-1930s, steel-framed backpacks, lightweight tents and sleeping bags, and Primus stoves all meant that individuals could spend two weeks on the trail without need of pack trains or guides. Very few new trails have been established since that time; of the few that have been cut, most have realigned or replaced existing trails for environmental reasons.

The Life of the Trail series divides historic routes through the Rockies into eight volumes, based primarily on geographical boundaries that influenced nineteenth-century travellers. Volumes are presented in order of entry by non-Aboriginal explorers, and routes within each volume are described in order of first use. Each book, designed to fit neatly into a pack, outlines the history of the routes in its region, giving modern-day travellers a feel for how they were established and who has used the trails since.

Life of the Trail 1 discusses historic routes and hikes in the area bounded by the North Saskatchewan River on the north and the Mistaya River, Bow River and Lake Minnewanka on the west and south. The most historically significant trip in this area was David Thompson's journey along the Red Deer River to meet the Kootenay Indians and take them back to Rocky Mountain House. Later, the Native route over Pipestone Pass to the Kootenay Plains was used extensively by tourist-explorers and mountaineers. Today this area is bounded by the David Thompson Highway (#11) in the north and the Icefields Parkway (#93), the Bow Valley Parkway (#1A) and Lake Minnewanka on the west and south.

The earliest fur-trade route across the Rockies was over Howse Pass. The trail is described in *Life of the Trail 2*, which presents the area bounded by the Kicking Horse River to the south; the Columbia Icefield to the north; and the Bow, Mistaya and North Saskatchewan rivers to the east. Later explorers created a popular return trip from the Kootenay Plains by adding the old Native trail down the Amiskwi River to the Howse Pass route. Also included in this volume are the Yoho Valley and the Castleguard Meadows. Today this area is bounded by the Trans-Canada Highway to the south and the Icefields Parkway to the east.

Life of the Trail 3 describes a single route. It follows the Bow River to Bow Pass, then the Mistaya, North Saskatchewan, Sunwapta and Athabasca rivers to the junction with the Miette. Today this is the route of the Trans-Canada Highway and Highway 1A to Lake Louise and the Icefields Parkway north to Jasper.

This book, *Life of the Trail 4*, details the history of three nineteenth-century fur-trade routes and one twentieth-century trail through what is now the southeastern section of Jasper National Park. The area is bounded by the North Saskatchewan River on the south and west, and by the Sunwapta and Athabasca rivers on the west and north. The fur-trade routes of Duncan McGillivray along the Brazeau River and Poboktan Creek, Jacques Cardinal along the southern boundary of Jasper National Park and on into the Job and Coral creek valleys, and Michael Klyne along Maligne Lake and on into the White Goat Wilderness, form the backbone of the trails in the area today. In the 1930s, Fred Brewster developed the Skyline Trail. Today the area is bounded by the David Thompson Highway (#11) in the south, the Icefields Parkway (#93) to the west and the Yellowhead Highway (#16) in the north.

With a little imagination, you will be able to tag along with those who have trodden these trails before. You can imagine Jacques Cardinal and his men herding horses along the remote valleys in the eastern part of Jasper National Park and the Earl of Southesk leading his colourful party of Métis and Native assistants along this route. Together with Professor Coleman and his party, you can follow Native guides over Job, Cataract and Jonas passes en route to the Sunwapta River. You can join Mary Schäffer, Mollie Adams, Billy Warren and Sid Unwin as they follow Poboktan Creek, searching for the creek that would lead them north to Maligne Pass and Lake.

You will also gain the information you need to follow in their footsteps. Over the years, the authors have hiked many of these trails together.

In the early twenty-first century, Emerson re-hiked each and every one of them to ensure the most accurate trail information possible. When we use the first person "I" in descriptions of adventures along the trails, we refer to Emerson and his experiences. We provide a complete trail guide for all routes, including those that do not fall within park boundaries, and have highlighted the trails on a topographic map. Carrying this lightweight book in your pack will enhance your backcountry experience so that as you slowly and strenuously climb The Notch on the Skyline Trail, for example, you can read about Fred Brewster's experience as he made his way over this pass for the first time, trying to find a route for his horses.

We hope that through these narratives, armchair travellers and backpackers alike will find a restful solitude in these remote valleys and join Mary Schäffer in feeling that:

> No one may know
> I went among those hills with a broken heart
> And only on the high places could I learn
> That I and mine
> Were very close together.
> We dare not tell those beautiful thoughts.
> They like to say "explorer" of me,
> No, only a hunter of peace.
> I found it.[1]

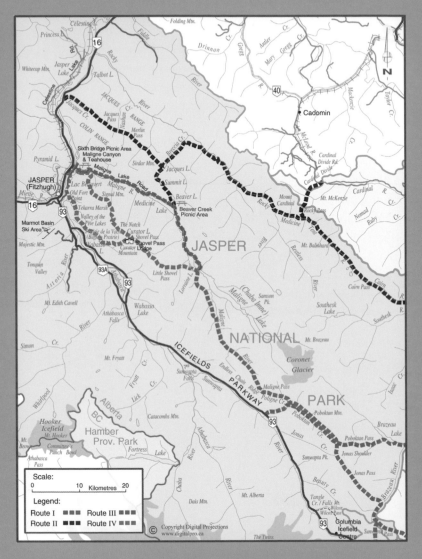

The northern area of Jasper National Park, east of the Icefields Parkway.

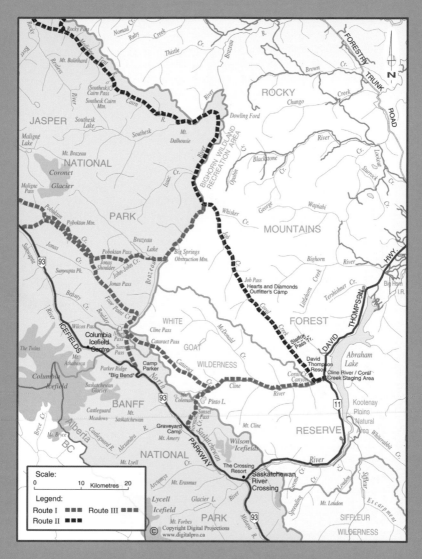

The area east of the Icefields Parkway and south of Maligne Lake to the North Saskatchewan River.

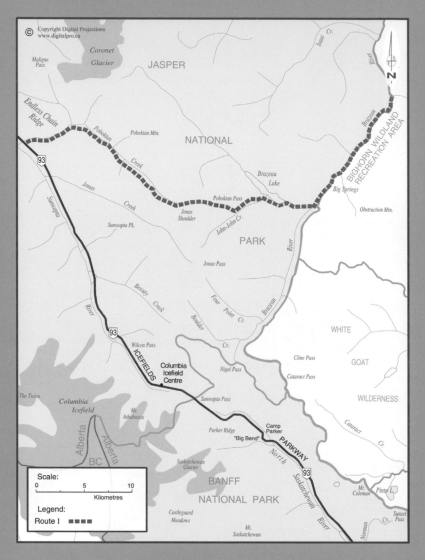

Duncan McGillivray's route from the Brazeau River to the Sunwapta River.

ROUTE I

The Fur Trade Heads West: Duncan McGillivray's Route from the Brazeau River to the Sunwapta

During the era of the tourist-explorer, outfitters wishing to provide their clients with the most "authentic" wilderness experience collaborated to limit contact between them and others on the trail. Over the course of thousands of kilometres on the trail, I have certainly had my times of solitude, but I have also had many rich encounters. I find that their common interest in being out on the trail tends to make backpackers friendly with one another; almost all will stop for a brief chat on the trail or in the campground. One unfortunate experience on the heavily used Brazeau Lake circuit, however, deepened my appreciation for the wisdom of the outfitters' ways.

I had begun the day's trek at Medicine Lake on today's South Boundary Trail and then joined McGillivray's route along the Brazeau River. I followed in his footsteps to Brazeau Lake and up the John-John Creek valley. It was late by the time I reached the top of Poboktan Pass, and the day's efforts had exhausted me. Having just spent five nights alone with the stars and the squirrels, it was a shock to arrive at the Jonas Cutoff Campsite to see 11 of the 13 sites occupied by a total of more than 30 people. I had known the site was a popular one and was aware that my solitude would be interrupted. But nothing in my past experience could have prepared for the general ambience I found there.

Three men entered the site at the same time I did. A quick look at the two vacant sites revealed that one was larger than the other, and I immediately suggested that I take the smaller one. One of the men grunted at me and dumped his backpack at the larger site. His two companions followed suit. None said a word. After setting up my camp, I took my food to the eating area. There were several picnic tables set up for the use of the campers, a luxury I had not previously experienced on this trip. All the tables were occupied, but one couple saw me coming and moved their equipment to one side to make room. They had finished eating and were relaxing over coffee. I tried unsuccessfully to engage them in conversation. Throughout the evening my attempts to interact with others in the campground met with similar polite but uninterested responses. For some reason, this particular campsite on this particular day was different from any that I had experienced in the backcountry. I felt uncomfortably alone amidst the crowds, much like on the sidewalks and parks in a big city.

Of course, when tourist-explorers did happen to meet up on the trail, it was often a highlight of their trip. So, too, many of my encounters. In fact, the very next summer, I camped with two friends at the very busy Four Point Campground, on the same Brazeau Lake circuit. Again there were a large number of campers, but the atmosphere was totally different. It was raining heavily, and we decided to cut our trip a day short and exit to the highway over Nigel Pass rather than take the Jonas Pass trail to the Jonas Campground. This meant that our car was many kilometres from our exit point. After setting up our tent, we each went our separate ways, talking to others in the campground. It did not take long to find campers willing to drive us from the Nigel Pass trailhead to the Poboktan Trail trailhead. A group of Americans who were heading home the next day offered us their canisters of bear spray and stove fuel, which they could not take on the plane with them. Although the site was crowded, the atmosphere was nothing like what I had experienced at Jonas Cutoff. It was more like a true backcountry experience.

Chronology

1800 North West Company fur trader Duncan McGillivray travels through the foothills to the Brazeau River and on to Brazeau Lake. He continues over Poboktan Pass and follows the creek to the Sunwapta River, making him the first recorded white man to travel in the Canadian Rockies north of the North Saskatchewan River.

1892 The Coleman brothers, Arthur and Lucius, travel from Morley through the foothills to the Brazeau River then follow McGillivray's trail to the Sunwapta. They continue down the Sunwapta to the Athabasca River, which they follow upstream to discover Fortress Lake.

1908 Mary Schäffer, Mollie Adams and Stewardson Brown, assisted by Billy Warren, Sid Unwin and Reggie Holmes, travel along McGillivray's old route from Brazeau Lake over Poboktan Pass. They turn north before reaching the Sunwapta and eventually reach Maligne Lake.

1914 Mrs. Crandell of Philadelphia and her companion, Mrs. Chandler, retrace Mary Schäffer's route to Maligne Lake with the assistance of Jack Greaves, Joe Woodworth and Jim Boyce.

1916 Jimmy Simpson, assisted by Jim Boyce and Ben Woodworth, leads a large group of hunters from the Campfire Club of New York over Nigel Pass and north over Jonas Pass, where they join the McGillivray route and follow it to Brazeau Lake.

1921 The Warden Service supervises the construction of a trail from the Sunwapta River along Poboktan Creek to Brazeau Lake.

1925 Caroline Hinman and guide Jim Boyce lead an Off the Beaten Track tour from Brazeau Lake over Poboktan Pass and north to Maligne Lake.

1933   Cliff Kopas and his wife, Ruth, join up with the Riviere party from the Waterton Lakes area to cross Nigel Pass en route to Brazeau Lake, where they join up with Warden Charlie Matheson and his wife, Mona. The pack train of 27 horses crosses Poboktan Pass and continues on to the warden cabin on the Sunwapta.

David Thompson is best known as a geographer, surveyor and map maker. This is an artist's depiction of what he looked like while surveying.

History

Fur Trade Explorers

In 1799, keen to expand their lucrative fur-trade networks, both the Hudson's Bay Company (HBC) and the North West Company (NWC, Nor'westers) built posts on the left bank of the North Saskatchewan River, just above the mouth of the Clearwater River. This was Peigan territory, but both companies were hoping these new forts – Acton House and Rocky Mountain House, respectively – would attract the trade of the Kootenays from west of the Rocky Mountains. It did not take long to realize that the Kootenays were unwilling to risk their lives at the hands of the Peigans by coming to the fort.

Undeterred, NWC officers decided to take their trade to the Kootenays, using Rocky Mountain House as a staging point. Duncan McGillivray, assigned to lead the company's first expedition across the mountains, was transferred to the Saskatchewan River fort, along with his assistant David Thompson.

Thompson was the first to arrive at the new post. In the fall of 1800, he led a group of Nor'westers and guides south to the Red Deer River, which they followed west into the mountains.[1] This is the first time European men are recorded to have entered the Canadian Rockies south of the Peace River area. When McGillivray, who arrived at Rocky Mountain House shortly after their return, heard Thompson's tales of this country to the south, he was anxious to see it for himself. Late in October 1800, the two men headed south to the Peigans' winter camp along the Highwood River. They returned to Rocky Mountain House on December 3.

The trip whetted McGillivray's appetite for adventure. He decided to pursue his objective of finding a transmountain route for the fur trade by taking an exploratory trip to the north and west. Unfortunately, by this point in his career, McGillivray had ceased to keep diaries of his travels, so few details are available of the journey that ushered the second period of exploration into the area north of the North Saskatchewan River and east of the Sunwapta–Athabasca corridor.

We know that McGillivray left Rocky Mountain House soon after December 3 with a Native guide, three men and several horses. They travelled eight miles (13 kilometres) west along the North Saskatchewan River then ventured overland through the foothills to the Brazeau River, perhaps intersecting the river along Opabin Creek.[2] They followed the Brazeau to Brazeau Lake then proceeded northwest along today's John-John Creek and over Poboktan Pass to Poboktan Creek.[3] The traders were the first European men to visit the Brazeau Lake area and likely the first to cross Poboktan Pass.

The McGillivray party proceeded to cross the chain of mountains that separates the sources of the Brazeau and Athabasca rivers (today's Endless Chain Ridge) via Poboktan Creek.[4] McGillivray and his men travelled four miles (six kilometres) down the Sunwapta River, which flows into the Athabasca. They then turned around and returned to Rocky Mountain House, the entire trip having taken about three weeks.

McGillivray intended to lead an expedition across the mountains the following spring, but it was not to be. A longstanding aliment – likely rheumatoid arthritis – flared up in February, preventing him from undertaking further travels. Thompson blamed the flare-up on the winter trip to the headwaters of the Brazeau River, claiming that McGillivray "took no precautions against the effect of exposure to the weather, wet feet, etc. [and] began to feel attacks of acute rheumatism, which became so violent as to oblige him to keep his bed."[5] The illness effectively ended Duncan McGillivray's explorations in the mountains; he retired to Montreal, where he died in 1808.

Opposite: The pathway along the North Saskatchewan River leads between the third and fourth forts built on the same location by the North West Company and the Hudson's Bay Company. The beauty of the location was likely lost on early fur traders, such as Duncan McGillivray and David Thompson.

Below: This restored fireplace, photographed in its original location, was part of the third or fourth fort at Rocky Mountain House, likely built in the period after 1835, after Duncan McGillivray had left the area.

Duncan McGillivray (circa 1770–1808)

Born in Scotland around 1770, McGillivray was destined for a life in the fur trade. His uncle, Simon McTavish, was a principal owner of the North West Company and generously paid to educate McGillivray for work with the company. In 1790 the young man followed his brother, William, to Montreal. McGillivray's apprenticeship began the following spring, with the expectation that he would be elected a partner within five to seven years. Thanks to the journal he kept during 1794–95, his career is best known for the time he spent at Fort George on the North Saskatchewan River.

Following that posting, McGillivray was indeed made a partner in the North West Company, and his journal writing ceased. In 1799 he journeyed to Montreal from the West, where he was made a partner in McTavish, Frobisher and Company, which owned a controlling interest in the North West Company. That winter, he made his way to Rocky Mountain House on the North Saskatchewan River in the foothills of Alberta.

He had planned to explore routes through the Rockies with David Thompson, but severe attacks of rheumatic fever forced him to curtail his explorations and eventually abandon the interior in 1802. He returned to McTavish, Frobisher and Company in Montreal and acted as their representative at the annual meetings in Kaministiquia (Thunder Bay, later Lakehead, Ontario). In 1803–1804, McGillivray unsuccessfully attempted to negotiate an alliance between the feuding Hudson's Bay Company and the North West Company; and in 1806 he bargained – again unsuccessfully – for an agreement that would allow the North West Company to ship furs out of Hudson Bay.

In the spring of 1808, as he suffered through the rheumatic fever that was to take his life, Duncan McGillivray managed to complete an essay: "Some account of the trade carried on by the North West Company." In it, he urged the British government to support the company's efforts to open up new avenues for the consumption of British manufactured goods by establishing trade beyond the Rocky Mountains.

McGillivray died in Montreal on April 9, 1808. There is no record of him having been married, but he probably had two children with a Native woman: a daughter Magdalene, born in 1801, and a son, William, who entered the fur trade in 1814.

A CENTURY LATER

Duncan McGillivray's trip was the only fur-trade expedition through this region, and his route remained untouched by European feet for nearly one hundred years. Even when the 1885 arrival of the railway in Banff, Laggan and Field initiated a steady stream of tourists, mountain climbers and explorers to the Rocky Mountains, very few travelled in the area north and east of the North Saskatchewan River – and many of those who did were hunters who did not record their trips.

Then the Coleman brothers ventured into the region. Arthur Philemon Coleman, professor of geology at the University of Toronto, had been intrigued by the controversy David Douglas initiated when he reported that the mountains on either side of Athabasca Pass (Mounts Hooker and Brown) rose to the towering heights of 17,000 feet (5182 metres). Coleman had previously attempted – unsuccessfully – to reach Athabasca Pass by canoeing down the Columbia River. He now felt that his best chance at success lay in travelling overland.

Coleman set about organizing his Mount Brown expedition for the summer of 1892, a much more ambitious trip than the Columbia River attempt. The party would consist of his brother:

> Mr. L. Q. Coleman, a rancher at Morley familiar with local conditions in the foot-hills, ... Mr. L. B. Stewart, Professor of Surveying in the University of Toronto, who had done some work in the west, ... Dr. Laird of Winnipeg, who was interested in mountains, and Mr. Pruyn, who knew something of horses and wished to join us as sportsman, assuring us that ... his rifle would help out our larder.[6]

Because they were to be passing through the hunting grounds of the Stoney people, they hired two band members as guides, "since one alone among white men was sure to get homesick and desert."[7] The guides were Jimmy Jacob, who spoke Cree and a bit of English, and Mark Two-young-men, a young lad who "spoke nothing which any of us could understand, but had a graceful and extensive command of the sign language."[8]

Lucius Coleman, a rancher from Morley, accompanied his brother on all of his overland trips. He is shown here with other founding members of the Alpine Club of Canada, on the far right in the second row.

The party assembled at the Coleman ranch on July 6, and by early evening all was packed and ready to go. The seven men and 13 cayuses the Colemans had purchased from the Stoneys headed north into the foothills on a well-beaten Stoney trail. Because the area had never been mapped, Stewart walked the entire distance using his pedometer to measure distances, sketching the hills and streams as he went along. The party continued through the foothills for five days then turned west along the Red Deer River. After some distance, they turned north, heading over Divide Pass to the Clearwater River and continuing north over Indianhead and Whiterabbit passes to the North Saskatchewan River, which they reached on July 16.[9]

Up to this point, their travels had been straightforward, if sometimes difficult. The guides were familiar with the 57 miles (92 kilometres) they had traipsed through traditional Stoney hunting grounds. Then, after two days of rest, badly needed by both horses and men, Jimmy Jacob:

led the way down stream to ford the Saskatchewan, where it was weakened by splitting into six branches with gravel bars between. Even so divided it was deep enough for us and reached the saddles on the horses' backs, so that most of us pulled off boots and socks and let the wooden stirrups float beside us. The water was muddy and the current strong, though steady and not dangerous.[10]

Two or three miles beyond the ford, they crossed the Cline River, which was much smaller but flowed more swiftly over rounded boulders, causing the ponies to lurch and slip.

As Jimmy Jacob was unfamiliar with the country beyond the Cline, Mark Two-young-men took over as lead guide. The easterners' expectation was that they would continue through the mountains to the Brazeau River, but Coleman reported that:

> with Mark Two-young-men riding jauntily ahead … instead of turning up one of the valleys, as we had hoped, he followed the Saskatchewan down, and passing the edge of the mountains, turned northwards along a wooded valley in the foot-hills. With the foot-hills came bad trail, for there were muskegs and soft ground along the creek and windfalls among the pine-groves to traverse.… The trail was fairly well marked, and in my capacity of *ogema* (chief) I deposed Mark from the leadership and sent Jimmy ahead once more.[11]

The trail the Colemans were following through the foothills was approximately the same route McGillivray had used some 92 years earlier. After three days, the party did indeed reach the Brazeau River. But realizing that they would never reach Athabasca Pass on their present course, Arthur Coleman took the situation into his own hands, heading upstream along the Brazeau back into the mountains. They later discovered that there were at least two passes (Job and Cataract) between the Saskatchewan and Brazeau that would have saved 40 miles (64 kilometres) of horrible trails.

Five miles (eight kilometres) into the mountains they halted. It was Sunday, and their companion, Pruyn, had become seriously ill. It seemed imperative to take him back to Morley, so Lucius Coleman and Jimmy Jacob set off on a three-hundred-mile (483-kilometre) round trip with a man so sick he could hardly sit on a horse. During their absence, the remaining members of the party moved only ten miles (16 kilometres) farther up the Brazeau. The presence of tepee poles leaning against a cliff a short distance away and sheep skulls and horns near an old campfire site indicated that their campsite had been previously used by the Stoneys. They spent the fortnight exploring the surrounding valleys and peaks.

On August 10, two weeks after their departure, Coleman and Jacob surprised the remaining party by coming down – rather than up – the valley of the Brazeau. They had travelled to the Saskatchewan via one new pass (Job Pass)[12] and returned by another (Cataract Pass),[13] both of which Jacob had heard of but had never crossed.

The reunited party set out along McGillivray's route, following the Brazeau River to the lake, travelling along its south shore for two or three miles (3 to 5 km), then turning southwest up a very steep and rugged little valley (John-John Creek valley) between:

> towering cliffs toward a pass we had seen on one of our climbs.... Crossing the barren pass next morning, we followed a creek flowing north-west toward a wide river valley which we had looked at longingly from a mountain-top some days before. We named the pass and creek Poboktan [Stoney for owl], from the big owls that blinked at us from the spruce trees.[14]

The following day they continued down Poboktan Creek into a wide, unknown valley. Coleman explained that:

> The new river was muddy though the weather was fine, so that there must be glaciers at its head, and in size it was nearly as large as the Bow at Morley; but it came from the

north-west instead of the north-east, so that it could not be the Whirlpool. On the other hand, it seemed too small for the Athabasca, and we decided to keep the Stony name, Sunwapta, at least for the present. Where to go next was the problem.[15]

This was new territory for the entire party, and Coleman continued to take the lead in determining their direction. They had unknowingly emerged from the Front Ranges into the valley of the Sunwapta and Athabasca rivers, north of the Columbia Icefield, and were observing the route of today's Icefields Parkway. Coleman led the party along the obvious route north down the Sunwapta, which soon flowed into the Athabasca. Without even being aware that white men had travelled there 92 years earlier, the Coleman party had retraced McGillivray's entire route!

The steep and rugged John-John Creek valley is visually enhanced by the unusual rock formations that grace its sides.

Above: The Athabasca River before the Sunwapta joins it. The trail to Fortress Lake is on the right at the bottom.

Opposite: After the death of her first husband, Mary Schäffer learned to camp and ride so that she could explore the Rocky Mountains between Lake Louise and Jasper.

They proceeded to follow the Athabasca upstream in a southerly direction, eventually discovering Fortress Lake. Obviously the stream they had followed was not the Whirlpool, which they knew from fur-trade records to flow northeast from Athabasca Pass. They would have to try to reach their destination again, another year.

The Colemans left the Fortress Lake area on August 29, retracing their route back along Poboktan Creek, over Poboktan Pass and on to Brazeau Lake and River to the campsite where they had waited for Lucius and Jimmy to return from taking Pruyn to Morley. "Here," Coleman explained, "instead of going north-east out of the mountains to the horrible trail in the foot-hills over which Mark had led us, we followed the route traversed by my brother and Jimmy in taking Pruyn to Morley."[16]

A QUEST

Sixteen more years passed before another party stumbled onto McGillivray's trail. In the fall of 1907, Philadelphian adventurer Mary Schäffer, her travelling companion Mollie Adams, and guides Billy Warren and Sid Unwin found themselves in the Kootenay Plains area after a full summer of exploring. They had heard of a major lake to the north and were anxious to find it.[17] After some convincing, Stoney Sampson Beaver, whose family had hunted in the area for many years and who had been taken to the lake as a young boy, drew Schäffer a map.[18]

The following year, Schäffer, Adams, Warren and Unwin were joined by botanist Stewardson Brown and packer–cook Reggie Holmes, 22 horses and a dog named Muggins. They followed the previous year's trail from Laggan along the Bow, Sunwapta and North Saskatchewan rivers

to Camp Parker, then they headed over Nigel Pass to Brazeau Lake. They followed McGillivray's and Coleman's footsteps over Poboktan Pass and along Poboktan Creek to a valley with several creeks running in from a more northerly direction.

Schäffer's party wondered which way to turn. Both McGillivray and Coleman had chosen to follow Poboktan Creek through the Endless Chain Ridge and into the valley that led to the Athabasca. But Schäffer's party was not privy to this information, and Beaver's rough map was of little assistance. After much agonizing, they made the wise decision to turn north, eventually arriving at Maligne Pass, which led them on to their destination: *Chaba Imne* or Maligne Lake.[19] Theirs was the first group recorded to have used Poboktan Pass since the Coleman trip of 1892.

A Philadelphian acquaintance, Mrs. Crandell, had planned to accompany Mary Schäffer on the 1908 trip that led to the "discovery" of Maligne Lake from the south, but illness forced her to withdraw. Reading *Old Indian Trails of the Canadian Rockies*, Schäffer's book describing her adventures of 1907 and 1908, rekindled Crandell's interest. In 1914 she and her companion, Mrs. Chandler, arranged with outfitter Jimmy Simpson to retrace the route. Jack Greaves was assigned to guide the trip, assisted by Joe Woodworth and Jim Boyce.

The party left Lake Louise on July 10 with five saddle horses, ten pack horses and provisions for six weeks. The trails were well-marked as far as Brazeau Lake. From then on, considerable trail-finding skills were required, as none of the party had previously travelled in the area. Fortunately, the guides had discussed the route with Billy Warren and Sid Unwin before heading out and had brought the map from *Old Indian Trails*. The trail along Coleman's 1892 route was faint, and they experienced some difficulty finding the creek that led north to Maligne Pass. But, with a great deal of assistance from Schäffer's map, they eventually succeeded in finding the route to Maligne Lake.[20]

The Brazeau River rises near the base of Cataract Pass and flows near the eastern slope of Nigel Pass on its northeasterly journey to the plains. This view looks northwest from near the top of Nigel Pass.

HUNTERS

The area near the top of Nigel Pass at the headwaters of the Brazeau River was one of Jimmy Simpson's favourite hunting grounds.[21] In 1915 he, Jim Boyce and Ben Woodworth led a large group of hunters into the area.[22] The men, members of the Campfire Club of New York, were a somewhat unusual group. Three of them – Dr. Harlow Brooks, a famous New York doctor; Joseph McAleenan, a diamond dealer; and John Murgatroyd, a New York businessman – were very experienced hunters. Brooks was anxious to bag a bighorn sheep and a grizzly bear, but the latter two planned to do most of their hunting with a camera so that "trophies could be carried home on film and plate, and the glad, strong, wild creatures still left to roam their beloved hills and peaks, and enjoy their right to life and happiness."[23] Two other friends, Ambrose Means and E. Sanborn, hoped to film the trip on an early version of a movie camera.

In late August, the Brooks party joined the pack train in Lake Louise and headed up the Bow Valley.[24] They crossed Nigel Pass on September 1 and dropped down into the valley of the Brazeau, headed for Jonas Pass. They continued over Jonas Shoulder and followed the McGillivray–Coleman route in reverse over Poboktan Pass to Brazeau Lake.[25] As they crossed Nigel Pass, they were hit with winter weather, which persisted for two weeks. Their hunting plans thwarted, they re-crossed Poboktan Pass on September 12, continued over Jonas Pass and returned to Lake Louise.

A FORMAL TRAIL

Nearly 30 years after the Coleman brothers' pioneering trip along this route, wardens cut a 53-mile (85-kilometre) trail. Beginning at the warden station at the junction of Poboktan Creek and the Sunwapta River, the trail followed Poboktan Creek to the pass then continued to Brazeau Lake and along the Brazeau River past the junction with Job Creek to its junction with the Southesk River. Under the supervision of Warden J.M. Christie, wardens marked the trail in the spring of 1921 and work crews followed. Construction was completed in 1922, transforming the McGillivray and Coleman route to the Job Creek junction into an important warden patrol route to the eastern ranges. It is still widely used by both wardens and backpackers.

Caroline Hinman was an enterprising woman who travelled widely throughout the Rocky Mountains leading lengthy escorted tours for eastern American teenaged girls. Three years after the warden trail was established, she led one of her Off the Beaten Track tours from Brazeau Lake over Poboktan and Maligne passes to Maligne Lake.[26] The party consisted of Hinman, her friend Lillian Gest, 12 young women, Jim Boyce and five helpers. The party would have required 19 saddle horses and likely an equal number of pack horses.

Hinman's usual practice was to travel several days until reaching a particularly beautiful spot, rest for two or three days then continue travelling. On this trip, which left Lake Louise on July 3, 1925, and returned on August 27, the group enjoyed a two-day layover on Job Pass before continuing to Brazeau Lake along the newly cut trail.[27] They arrived at the lake on July 19 then continued to follow McGillivray's route over Poboktan Pass. Then they headed north on Old Klyne's Trail, reaching Maligne Pass on July 21.[28] They spent three days at Maligne Lake before proceeding to Jasper.

Lillian Gest spent 63 consecutive summers in the Canadian Rockies, often accompanying her friend, Caroline Hinman, on her Off the Beaten Track tours and hunting trips.

Caroline Hinman (1884–1966)

Shortly after her 1906 graduation from Massachusetts's Smith College, Caroline Hinman accepted a college friend's invitation to travel to California to be her bridesmaid. Little did she know this trip would set the course for the next 50 years of her life. She ended up spending three months in California and another two travelling back to the east coast. The journey had awakened her strong desire to travel and explore the world.

Hinman was born in Cincinnati, Ohio, on November 8, 1884. Six years later, her family moved to Chatham, New Jersey, then two years later to nearby Summit, Hinman's home base for the remainder of her life. She took her first trip to Europe in 1909. The following year, she agreed to guide four friends on a similar tour. She discovered she had much more of an appetite for guiding than for being led.

In 1913 Hinman travelled to the Canadian Rockies to visit friends Bess and Albert MacCarthy on their British Columbia ranch. Accomplished climbers, the MacCarthys introduced Hinman to the Alpine Club of Canada's summer camp. After the camp, renowned outfitter Curly Phillips escorted Hinman on a trip north of Mount Robson. She was hooked. She joined Phillips on a similar trip the following year then organized her own trip to the American Rockies in 1916. In 1917 she led her first all-Canadian trip in the Rockies.

In her early years of guiding, Caroline worked full-time as secretary to the Board of Education in Summit, NJ. By 1921 she had left the position to dedicate herself entirely to her guiding business. Hinman's Off the Beaten Track tours generally catered to wealthy American teenaged girls, though she did occasionally lead mixed groups of all ages. She returned to the Canadian Rockies nearly every summer for the next 40 years, conducting up to three guided trips a season. Supplementing her income from these excursions by guiding winter tours overseas, Hinman was able to make a good living – and have some fun! Between the end of touring season in the Rockies and her winter tours overseas, she often hunted in the Rockies with friends.

As time went on, Hinman took advantage of the changes that were taking place in the mountains. She became a member of the Trail Riders of the Canadian Rockies, attended many of their camps and served on the executive. After Skoki Lodge was completed in the early 1930s, she led a four-week excursion, guiding day trips from the comfort of the lodge. Later, she led a four-week car trip from Banff to Jasper on the newly completed motor road and a three-week horseback excursion followed by a Peace River boat trip organized by her friend, Curly Phillips.

By 1929 Hinman had started hiring former campers to lead her trips in the Rockies, freeing her to lead more exotic trips in various places around the world. In 1932–33 she escorted a six-month, around-the-world trip. But her various trips and tours did not prevent Hinman from becoming heavily involved in many civic and welfare projects in her home town of Summit, NJ, including volunteer work with Overlook Hospital, the Red Cross, the Summit Convalescent Home for Children, the Summit Playhouse Association and the Unitarian Church. At the age of 74, she finally decided to retire. She lived quietly in her home town for the next six years, until her death on July 12, 1966.

In 1931 Hinman summed up her life for her college reunion book as follows:

As I look back over the past twenty-five years I feel I have accomplished very little. I have no husband, I have no children, I have no home of my own, I have written no books, I have amassed no fortune, I have distinguished myself in no way whatsoever ... but I have been extremely happy, extremely busy, utterly contented and absorbed in my job of taking people to out-of-the-way places in the world ... I might have done better – and I might have done worse.[29]

Caroline Hinman toured extensively throughout the Canadian Rockies, leading her Off the Beaten Track tours for young American girls. Outfitter Jim Boyce nicknamed her "Timberline Kate" because of her penchant for choosing campsites high on mountain sides or on a pass, in order to enjoy a good view.

WESTWARD BOUND

One of the more unusual groups to use the McGillivray–Coleman route from Brazeau Lake to the Sunwapta River crossed Poboktan Pass in 1933. In the midst of the Great Depression, Cliff and Ruth Kopas had just been married in the southern Alberta foothills. Between them they owned five horses and had cash reserves of $2.65! Nevertheless, they decided to set off for the Pacific Coast. They left in June, following an indirect route that allowed them to see the major beauty spots of the Canadian Rockies. They proceeded from Calgary to the Bow River via Mount Assiniboine and Sunshine Meadows, and then they travelled up Redearth Creek and on to Lake Louise. From there they followed the Bow River to the North Saskatchewan.[30] At the junction of the Saskatchewan and Alexandra rivers, they met up with another party heading toward Jasper.

The Riviere party, a group of professional outfitters from the Waterton Lakes region of southern Alberta, was headed for the goldfields of the Cariboo in British Columbia, where they hoped to start anew in the outfitting business. The party consisted of George, the leader; his wife, Maggie; her sister, Annie Clark; and two men, Ray Cyrl from Waterton Lake and Slim Black from Banff. Upon George Riviere's suggestion, the two parties decided to travel together from Graveyard Camp to Jasper. [31] The 21-horse pack train got underway the next day, winding its way up the Saskatchewan to Camp Parker, at the junction of the Nigel Pass trail. They spent two nights at the camp before proceeding over Nigel Pass to the headwaters of the Brazeau River, which they followed to Brazeau Lake. That evening, they camped near the warden cabin on the Brazeau where they met Warden Charlie Matheson and his wife, Mona (nee Harragin).[32]

The Mathesons, who were also headed to Jasper, decided to join the other two parties, making a pack train of 27 horses strung out over a quarter mile along the old McGillivray–Coleman trail. The combined parties spent their first night at the Mathesons' Waterfall Warden Cabin on Poboktan Creek then proceeded along Poboktan Creek to their home cabin at its junction with the Sunwapta.

The entire party stayed a day to rest the horses and an additional three to wait out a rainstorm. Days were spent repairing equipment and completing other chores; evenings in the Mathesons' hospitable trail home singing, playing games and making plans for the future. Despite the ravages of the Depression, this was an optimistic group of young people, and everyone seemed to dream of a dude ranch with a lakeside cabin boasting a beautiful view and a big fireplace.

By the fifth day, it was back to reality. The weather had cleared, allowing them to proceed north to Jasper, where the parties separated.[33] Four months later, the Kopases reached the Pacific at Bella Coola and found that the Bella Coola valley fulfilled all of their dreams. Unfortunately, the dream did not last long. Sixteen months later, Ruth died of complications during childbirth. Ruth's sister and husband adopted baby Keith, who grew up with them in Calgary, leaving Cliff alone in Bella Coola. He spent the rest of his days there, until his death in 1978.

Warden Charlie Matheson (r), shown here with outfitter Curly Phillips and Charlie's wife, Mona (nee Harragin). Matheson patrolled the backcountry in the Brazeau Lake region for many years. After their marriage, Mona joined in his pursuits.

The Trail Today

Duncan McGillivray's party approached the Brazeau River from the east and proceeded along the river, over Poboktan Pass and along Poboktan Creek to the Sunwapta River. Somewhere along the Sunwapta, they turned around and retraced their steps back to Rocky Mountain House. We have described the trail for the return trip as there is no easy approach from the east. Today Poboktan Pass is part of a very popular backpacking circuit from Nigel Pass to Brazeau Lake and back over the Poboktan and Jonas passes.

The route up Poboktan Creek stays mainly in the trees until the junction with the Maligne Lake trail.[34] This is a historic junction, where the Schäffer party had to make a serious decision as to which direction to take. Several valleys converge here, and we encourage hikers to pause and reflect on the scene as viewed through the eyes of Mary Schäffer and her party. The trail they arrived on is a very pleasant hike along Poboktan Creek. Jasper Park's three campgrounds in the next 20 kilometres permit hikers who desire to proceed at a leisurely pace – though the campground at Jonas Cutoff is on the very popular tourist Brazeau Lake backpack circuit and is often fully booked during July and August.

From the campground, the approach to Poboktan Pass is quite steep but well worth the effort. The top of the pass is beautiful and portions of the trail's continuation down the John-John Creek valley are spectacular. Views of Brazeau Lake increase in grandeur as the trail nears the lake. The lake itself is reached off a side trail; many hikers will want to spend some time in this area.

Continuing west, the very pleasant trail follows the Brazeau River valley. The first spectacular natural feature is at Big Springs, where a large volume of water bubbles and boils out of the side of a mountain, flooding the area below. After viewing this natural phenomenon, hikers proceed along the valley, which becomes more beautiful as it follows the river, at times skirting meadows. Shortly after the Isaac Creek Campground and Warden Cabin, McGillivray and his party would have forded the Brazeau River and continued through the foothills. There is no trail along that part of their route today and fording the Brazeau River is normally not an option for hikers.

There are no route-finding difficulties along McGillivray's route through the Front Ranges and only one steep pass. The route offers spectacular scenery on Poboktan Pass and in the John-John Creek valley, other very scenic areas along Poboktan Creek and the Brazeau River valley, and the grandly beautiful Brazeau Lake. These features combined make it a suitable hike for hikers of all ages, although parents of young children will have to allow sufficient time for young ones to traverse the pass.

It is largely a one-way hike, with the only option of starting from the east being the Job Pass–South Boundary Trail routes – both rather arduous hikes.[35] Hikers can join the trail mid-route by taking Nigel Pass and following the Brazeau River to the lake or by crossing Jonas Pass and Jonas Shoulder. From the north, the route can be approached from Maligne Pass, and any of these options can be used as alternative return routes if transportation has been arranged.

The water at Big Springs stems from a subterranean source whose outflow gushes profusely from the side of the mountain, flooding the area below.

Trail Guide

Distances are adapted from existing trail guides: Patton and Robinson, Potter, and Beers, and from Gem-Trek maps. Distances intermediate from those given in the sources are estimated from topographical maps and from hiking times. All distances are in kilometres.

From the Sunwapta River over Poboktan Pass and along the Brazeau River

Maps   83 C/6 Sunwapta Peak
            83 C/7 Job Creek

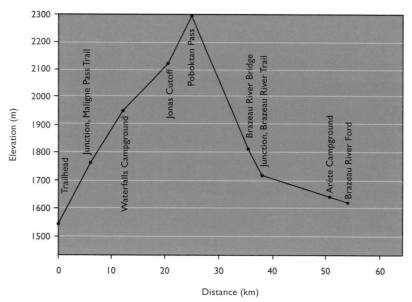

Trailhead

The west end of the trailhead is located on the Icefields Parkway (# 93), 17.5 km south of the Sunwapta Falls junction and 31.5 km north of the Icefields Centre. The parking lot is 0.2 km south of the Sunwapta Warden Station, just beyond Poboktan Creek on the east side of the highway.

From the east, the trail can be approached along the Cardinal–Southesk route up Jacques Creek.[36]

0.0 Poboktan Creek parking lot.

0.1 Cross to the north side of the creek on a steel bridge and continue along a wide, well-used trail. The trail follows the creek and you soon come to a beautifully made log bench. The trail then climbs through the forest away from the creek.

5.4 Trail returns to the creek with pleasant views of the mountains then veers off into the forest again.

6.2 Trail junction. Maligne Pass trail goes to the left (north). Continue ahead (east).

6.4 Cross Poligne Creek on a bridge. Continue on a good trail through the forest.

7.5 Poboktan Creek Campground. Just beyond the campground, a major stream comes in from the left (north) and splits into two, with bridges across both sections. Continue through the forest on a good trail and cross a bridge over a side stream coming in from the left (north). When you reach a pole fence and gate, cross another bridged creek.

12.0 Waterfalls Campground. Continue along the valley-bottom trail.

13.6 Waterfalls Warden Cabin. Continue through a largely treed area with frequent good views.

14.2 Bridged side stream. The trail continues along the side of the Poboktan Creek valley. The terrain is quite open and very beautiful.

19.7 Sign in a tree pointing left to the McCready horse camp. Continue ahead (southeast), passing an old campground that has been closed.

21.3 Jonas Cutoff Campground. Cross two bridged streams.

24.3   Poboktan Pass. A very beautiful area. From the top of the pass, the trail drops steeply through a fairly open area.

28.6   John-John Creek Campground. Shortly after the campground, there is a bridge across the creek. Do not cross. Stay on the left (north) side of the creek. Continue downhill through the narrow and very beautiful John-John Creek valley. There are numerous avalanche paths as you proceed, affording great views – especially looking back toward the pass.

32.8   John-John Creek bridge. Cross the bridge and come to a large alluvial fan on the floodplain of John-John Creek. Partway along, you will catch a good view of Brazeau Lake. The trail climbs over a high ridge then drops down toward the lake.

36.5   Northwest Brazeau River bridge. This bridge crosses to the east of the fast-flowing, wide outflow from Brazeau Lake. After crossing the bridge, the Brazeau River Bridge Campground is on the left (north). Continue to the right (east).

38.6   Junction. The trail to Nigel Pass branches to the right (southwest). Keep left (northeast) on the South Boundary Trail, which heads northeast along the Brazeau River. In a short distance, pass through a gate across the trail.

*   For those hikers using the McGillivray route to exit the Cardinal–Southesk route (Route II below), take the Nigel Pass trail to the right (southwest) along the Brazeau River as far as the Four Point Campground (15.6 km). This is a pleasant valley hike along the Brazeau River on a well-defined trail. From the Four Point Campground, hikers can follow Old Klyne's Trail over Nigel Pass (Route III below).

39.0   Brazeau Campground and Warden Cabin. Just beyond there is another gate across the trail and the Brazeau Meadows horse camp. The trail splits, with the hiker trail staying on higher ground to the left (north). After rejoining the horse trail, the trail stays close to the river and passes through a stand of cottonwood trees.

42.5   Big Springs. Streams gush out of the side of the rock, forming springs and flooding the meadow below. Continue along the scenic Brazeau River valley.

46.7   Trail crosses a large grass meadow in a particularly beautiful area then, by way of a bridge, crosses a rushing stream. Continue through a wooded area into a burned area then back into fairly open forest.

51.2   Arête Campground. Shortly after the campground is the Arête Warden Cabin. The trail continues along the Brazeau River in a northeasterly direction, often in the woods.

53.6   The trail turns to the north, avoiding a small meadow followed by a pond on the left.

        This is the end of McGillivray's trail. Near where the trail turns north, he would have crossed the Brazeau River to the east and continued into the foothills to the southeast. There is no trail today along McGillivray's route through the foothills. Crossing the Brazeau River in this area is not usually an option for hikers.

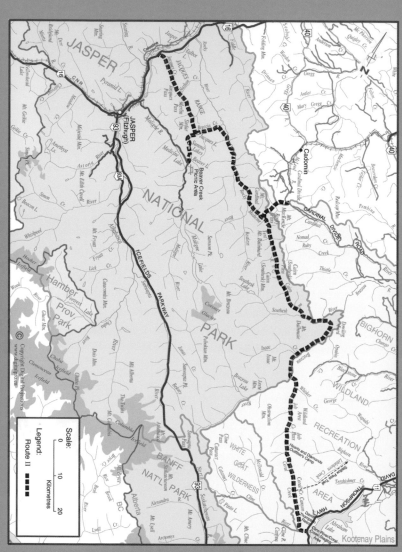

The Jacques Cardinal–Earl of Southesk route from the Athabasca River to the North Saskatchewan River over Southesk and Job passes.

ROUTE II

Horses and Hunters: The Jacques Cardinal–Earl of Southesk Route from the
Athabasca to the North Saskatchewan Rivers over Southesk and Job Passes

I could have hiked the Rocky Pass exit to the Cardinal Divide – the route the Earl of Southesk used to enter the Front Ranges from the foot-hills – by adding another day to my eight-day loop hike from Medicine Lake along the South Boundary Trail to Maligne Lake. Instead, I chose to drive Highway 40 from Hinton to the coal mining town of Luscar then proceed to the Cardinal Divide along what was at times an exceed-ing rough and twisting road through a coal mine. The heavy haulers on a parallel road – which made my VW Westphalia Van look like a toy – were, to say the least, intimidating.

My hike over Rocky Pass to the Medicine Tent River was unevent-ful. As has been the case on many of my outings, I had not seen another person since I left the semi-civilized area – in this case, the coal mines. Since this was a simple in-and-out day hike, I did not linger at the river but immediately began my return trip along the same route. The top of the pass was above treeline and therefore very open, although there were small clumps of dwarfed spruces scattered in protected spots. A snow squall had blown in while I was crossing the pass, gusting directly in my face, and I was walking with my head down to keep the snow out of my eyes, blissfully immersed in my own world. Partway across the pass, I subconsciously detected some movement ahead of me and immediately stopped to look up. Directly in front of me was a large grizzly standing on its hind legs, looking at me.

My first thought was: what a wonderful photo for our book. On second thought, still thinking about photography, I decided that I did not want to get my camera wet in the blowing snow and that the snow would likely prevent getting a good shot anyway. My third thought was that this was the only trail in the area, it was the only way out of here and that bear was blocking my way. Fortunately, I had no time to reflect on that situation. The bear, likely having satisfied himself that I was just a human on the trail, and perhaps having decided that I was too old and tough to make a good meal, dropped to all fours and wandered off on his way, leaving me free to advance.

Because the rolling terrain prevented me from seeing where the bruin had meandered, there was still an element of danger to proceeding along the trail. I took out my pepper spray, removed the safety catch and continued cautiously, watching carefully for any movement. This was the first time I had hiked with the pressurized canister in my hand. Even though the bear behaved in a predictable manner for a situation far from civilization, carrying the spray in hand seemed prudent at the time. Fortunately, I did not see the bear again.

Rocky Pass is a high windswept gap that separates the Cardinal Divide from the Medicine Tent River. This well-named pass provides the only access to the remote valley between Jacques Lake to the north and the Southesk River to the south.

Chronology

1820s   Jacques Cardinal herds horses up Jacques Creek, south along Rocky River to the Brazeau and likely over Job Pass to the Kootenay Plains.

1859   James Carnegie, the flamboyant Earl of Southesk, enters the trail along the Medicine Tent River by crossing Rocky Pass from the Cardinal Divide area. He continues south to the Brazeau River and over Job Pass to the Saskatchewan.

1884   J.J. McArthur, working for the Topographical Survey of Canada, surveys part of Cardinal's old route along the Southesk River.

1892   The Coleman brothers use the route over Job Pass on their return trip from Fortress Lake.

1898   Geologist James McEvoy retraces Cardinal's route up Jacques Creek, east to the Rocky River and on to the Brazeau. He concludes that Native people had travelled the route many years earlier.

1925   Caroline Hinman leads an Off the Beaten Track tour north from the Saskatchewan River, over Job Pass to the Brazeau River and on to Brazeau Lake.

1926   Caroline Hinman leads another tour north from the Saskatchewan, this time going farther east in the foothills to join the old Cardinal trail north of Rocky Pass. They follow Cardinal's route as far as Jacques Lake then travel west to Medicine Lake.

1930   Mona Harragin, one of the first female licensed guides in Jasper National Park, leads a pack train from Brazeau Lake north along Cardinal's route to Jacques Lake and on to Medicine Lake.

1937   Warden Ed McDonald breaks his pelvis when thrown from his horse while patrolling the old Cardinal trail. It takes him three days to crawl to the nearest cabin with a telephone and a monumental effort to reach the phone mounted high on the wall.

History

Early Travellers

The South Boundary Trail through today's Jasper National Park is a peaceful trail through several seldom-visited valleys along the eastern ranges of the Rocky Mountains. Its first recorded traveller was Jacques Cardinal, a colourful Métis mountain man and fur trader.[1] In the 1820s, Cardinal tended horses for the Hudson's Bay Company in the Athabasca valley, herding them over mountain passes and through remote valleys to the Kootenay Plains for the traders. The mountain range northeast of the Merlin Pass trail, the Jacques Range, was named for him, as were Jacques Lake and Jacques Pass. Farther east, the Cardinal River was also named after the fur trader, with several other features taking their names from the river.[2]

In 1898 geologist James McEvoy retraced Cardinal's route up Jacques Creek and over Merlin Pass to Jacques Lake and east along Breccia Creek to the Rocky River and the Brazeau. He found the trail scattered with artifacts suggesting that Native people had travelled the route many years earlier – likely on their way over Job Pass to the North Saskatchewan River and east along the river to Rocky Mountain House.[3] His findings suggest that Jacques Cardinal was likely following an old Native trail, perhaps even led by Native guides.

In his 1917 book, *Description of and Guide to Jasper Park*, M.P. Bridgland mentions the trail up Jacques Creek and over Merlin Pass, describing it as: "an old trail [which] leads to Jacques Lake, about fifteen miles to the southeast. It is used very little and is not widely known. It crosses the summit of Jacques creek and two other summits before reaching Jacques Lake."[4] There is no other early description of portions of Cardinal's old route along the Rocky, Medicine Tent and Cairn rivers to the Brazeau. And, in spite of the fact that J.J. McArthur surveyed along the Southesk River portion of Cardinal's route in 1884 as part of his work for the Topographical Survey of Canada, neither is there any other record of early travels over Job Pass to the North Saskatchewan.

J.J. McArthur, a surveyor with the Topographic
Survey of Canada, surveyed part of Southesk's
route in 1884. The task required scaling many
mountains with his partner, W.S. Drewry (above).

53

A HUNTER'S PARADISE

The portion of today's South Boundary Trail south of Rocky Pass on the Medicine Tent River has the honour of having been described by James Carnegie, the flamboyant and eccentric Earl of Southesk. The Earl arrived in Canada in 1859 for an extended hunting trip, which he hoped would improve his health and help him recover from the recent death of his young wife.[5] His trip began at Fort Garry (today's Winnipeg, Manitoba). A leisurely trip across the prairies ensued – the highlight being the opportunity to participate in a buffalo hunt shortly after crossing the South Saskatchewan River. By the time the Southesk party reached Fort Edmonton, it consisted of ten men: Métis guide Antoine Blandoine, Red River guide John Mackay, Red River Scotsmen Donald Matheson and Morrison M'Beath, French Métis George Kline from Fort Garry, Scots-Métis Piskan Munroe and James Short, Highlander Duncan Robertson (who had accompanied Southesk from Scotland), Iroquois Toma (Thomas Ariwakenha) and French Métis hunter Lagrace.

After a week at the fort, they abandoned their wagons in favour of pack saddles and headed west along the route of today's Highway 16. They were one of the first groups to use this route; most of their contemporaries were travelling north from Edmonton to Fort Assiniboine on the Athabasca River. The Earl planned to travel west as far as Jasper – making him the first tourist in what is now Jasper National Park – then make his way south through the mountains to the Kootenay Plains. A chance meeting with Henry Moberly (of Jasper House) at Lac Ste. Anne significantly altered these plans. Moberly suggested that Southesk travel only as far as the McLeod River then head south and west toward its headwaters, where he could enter the mountains over a narrow rocky pass (Rocky Pass). He warned that game was scarce in the Athabasca Valley and enticed Southesk with the suggestion that no white man had ever crossed from the McLeod River to the North Saskatchewan.

Eleven days after leaving Fort Edmonton, Southesk caught his first glimpse of the Rocky Mountains:

James Carnegie, Ninth Earl of Southesk (1827–1905)

James Carnegie was born in Edinburgh, Scotland, on November 16, 1827, to Sir James Carnegie, Fifth Baronet, and Charlotte Lysons. His privileged position as a nobleman of considerable means allowed him to be educated at Edinburgh Academy. He then trained at Sandhurst, was commissioned in the Gordon Highlanders and transferred to the Grenadier Guards.

After succeeding his father as the Earl of Southesk in 1849, he retired from the armed forces and devoted his efforts to re-building the family seat: Kinnaird Castle, Brechin. That same year, Southesk married Lady Catherine Hamilton Noel, daughter of Charles Noel, First Earl of Gainsborough. They had one son and at least one daughter. After only six years of marriage, Lady Catherine died in 1855. Southesk's effort to recover from the loss of his young wife was an important factor in his decision to take a pleasure trip across Canada in 1859–60.

Southesk was a passionate sportsman with a keen taste for adventure and a reputation for shooting at anything wild that moved. His collection of hunting guns comprised a very impressive armoury. He diligently pursued rarer species and went to great lengths to preserve his trophies and ship them back home. Though he travelled entirely for pleasure, Southesk was also an ardent observer of the country through which he travelled. His book, *Saskatchewan and the Rocky Mountains*, published in Scotland in 1875, meticulously reports his observations.

Shortly after his 1860 return to Scotland, Southesk married Susan Catherine Mary Murray, the eldest daughter of the Sixth Earl of Dunmore. In total the Earl had at least nine children from his two marriages. He was a member of the British House of Lords and spent much time managing his vast agricultural estate. In later life, he gained acclaim as a Shakespearian scholar, and as an author and poet. He collected antique gems, old masters, books and other antiquities to adorn his home, Kinnaird Castle. To these items he added trophies and other Native artifacts collected on his North American travels. He died at home in February 1905.

James Carnegie, Earl of Southesk, came to Canada on a pleasure trip to regain his health and to partake in the "sport" of shooting wild animals. His arsenal of fine weapons was put to good use on the trail, often shooting more animals than his party could use for food, leaving the carcasses for predators.

A glorious sight opened upon my view – the Rocky
Mountain range, stretching along the horizon as far as the
eye could reach. Below us rolled the river among dark pines;
hills, also covered with pines ... filled up the prospect for
many miles; then came flat bare eminences, the footstools
of the loftier range, and then uprose the mountains themselves, rugged in form, peaked and tabled, and scored with
gashes, – not magnified hills, but rocks in the very arche-
type. Too remote to display any smaller modulations, they
rose flat against the blue sky, themselves all steeped in a
soft mellow gray from summit to base; ... and on some of
the high shoulders of the greater peaks, spots and masses
of snow glittering in the sun.[6]

Blandoine proceeded to lead the party through the very rugged Cardinal
Divide area and over today's Rocky Pass to the Medicine Tent River.
Although they did not know of the earlier traveller and no signs of his

The hike over Rocky Pass begins at the
Cardinal Divide area in the eastern foothills.
The Cadomin access road can be seen in the
centre of the photo.

On a clear day, the cairn on top of Southesk Cairn Mountain (left) can still be seen from the trail.

trail would have remained, they were now on Jacques Cardinal's old route, which they would follow to the Kootenay Plains.

After travelling a short distance south along the Medicine Tent River, the party stopped to set up camp. They stayed a few days, during which time Southesk climbed a mountain and erected a cairn in honour of the first European to visit the valley: himself. "I am the first European who has visited this valley," Southesk declared, "and if I might have the geographical honour of giving my name to some spot of earth, I should choose the mountain near which the two rivers rise."[7] Today the mountain is indeed known as Southesk Cairn Mountain.

A short distance along the trail, Southesk paused to observe the scene:

> Antoine and I rode forward together, but stopping for a
> while at the turn of the hill, we heard the rest of the party
> approaching, and waited for their arrival. As my men came
> into view, dashing up at a brisk pace or galloping here and
> there to drive in the straggling horses, I was greatly struck

with their picturesque appearance; having, indeed, hardly seen them on the march together since we left Edmonton, for the thick woods and narrow winding tracks keep a large party always in detachments.[8]

One of the Earl's main objectives was to engage in what he referred to as "good sport ... among the larger animals."[9] He brought an arsenal of firearms, which he generally used to shoot at anything that moved. At their camping spot on the North (Cairn) River, four miles (six kilometres) beyond the mountain, Southesk and his companions managed to obtain some excellent trophies from a herd of bighorn sheep. Although a party of 11 men would require a large amount of meat for survival, Southesk and his men often got carried away in a needless slaughter, killing far more animals than they could use either as trophies or for food. The Earl apparently had second thoughts about the needless killing, writing:

> There is something repugnant to the feelings in carrying death and anguish on so large a scale amongst beautiful inoffensive animals. One thinks little – too little – of the killing of small game, but in shooting large game the butchery of the act comes more home, one sees with such vividness the wounds, and the fear, and the suffering. But it does not do to look at things too narrowly, – one grows morbid, – and no thinking will ever bring one to the root of the matter.[10]

Carrying on with their journey, the men traversed a low pass to the Cairn River. The Cairn runs into today's Southesk River, which led them south to the main east–west river in the region: the Brazeau. It was then that Southesk made the unfortunate discovery that Blandoine was not familiar with the region. Intent on leaving the mountains by the shortest route, the guide began heading east along the Brazeau. Though others supported his efforts, Southesk wanted to continue in the mountains by the "finer and less-traversed routes."[11] Eventually he prevailed, and the party turned upstream back into the mountains.

Job Creek and its delightful valley. This view looks north from partway up the valley.

Above: Southesk and his large party somehow missed the very obvious Job Pass, probably by travelling too far up Job Creek, which veers to the south. Crossing the mountain range took all of the skills the men could muster.

Opposite: The view down the Coral Creek valley from near the top of Job Pass brought great joy to the Southesk party after a very difficult crossing of the divide.

After some distance, they headed south along a stream entering the Brazeau: today's Job Creek. Following the stream to its headwaters, they somehow missed turning off on a rather obvious pass that would have taken them into the drainage of today's Coral Creek. Southesk explained that "Lagrace had a general idea of the road, but he found himself at fault when we suddenly came to a mountain which stood right across our path, apparently forbidding farther progress, for it was no better than a chaos of rocks and great broken stones."[12]

While his men tried to find a pass that would lead them over this obstacle, Southesk went hunting. He returned to find that

> M'Kay had got all the horses to the top of the hill by a path that seemed quite impracticable, for it was not only exceedingly steep, but composed of very sharp many-cornered

blocks, much the size of a cart, lying at different levels, – near one another, but sufficiently apart to leave great deep holes between, where knife-like smaller stones did not fill the openings. At the summit was a nearly perpendicular wall of hard frozen snow, about twenty feet high. Steps were cut, and the horses dragged up with ropes.[13]

Their troubles did not end at the top of this mountain, as the route down the other side initially appeared impassable. However, Southesk pointed out that "near the snow on our left ... appeared a lower ridge, and this was our only hope, for unless fortunate enough to pass over it and arrive at some other valley, we had no choice but to go back, losing several days and all the heavy toil of men and horses."[14] They were in luck.

The ridge, although steep, was in time ascended, and to our great joy there was a practicable road down a watercourse [Coral Creek] on the other side; ... by evening we found ourselves comfortably encamped at the side of a mountain stream which evidently flowed towards the Saskatchewan, the direction in which we had intended to travel.[15]

Southesk had great expectations that Coral Creek would lead his party to the Saskatchewan. Although he did not comment on the scenery, the Job and Coral creek valleys are among the most beautiful in the Front Ranges.

Their trip downstream along Coral Creek to the end of Jacques Cardinal's old route at the Kootenay Plains was uneventful. After managing to cross the North Saskatchewan River on a raft, they realized that it was now September 19 and they were still some distance from the prairie. Eventually they found a good trail leading south: the Pipestone Pass–Siffleur River route to the Bow River, which Southesk called the "Bow River Road."[16] They exited the mountains along the Bow River, reaching Old Bow Fort on September 30. [17] All – including Southesk – were happy to be out of the mountains.

ADVENTURES IN THE FRONT RANGES

Although Southesk's trip along part of today's South Boundary Trail and over Job Pass to the North Saskatchewan River was published as an adventure story in 1875, the book did not entice other explorers, adventurers or mountaineers into the area. In fact, early travellers tended to ignore the entire eastern side of the Rocky Mountains. The exception to this rule were the Coleman brothers, whose apparent ignorance of Southesk's trip and book did not prevent them from using the eastern Rockies as their entry point into the mountains. Their 1892 trip along the Brazeau River, which essentially retraced North West Company fur trader Duncan McGillivray's early trip, is described in Route I above.

Although the initial approach to the Brazeau was made on a terrible trail through the foothills, Stoney Jimmy Jacob guided Lucius Coleman along another trail he had heard of – over Job Pass and down Coral Creek – when they had to return to Morley with an ill trailmate. This was Jacques Cardinal's route to the Kootenay Plains, which Southesk had also followed. When it came time for the entire Coleman party to head back to Morley at the end of the summer, they decided to use the new route over Job Pass.

In Coleman's words:

> First we went south, along a stream which we called Job's Creek, from the enterprising Stony Indian Job Beaver, who had worked out the trail, then climbed a steep slope to Job's Pass, rising above eight thousand feet, a thousand feet above timber-line. From this rough mountain saddle an equally steep descent leads to an important stream flowing into Cataract Creek [Cline River] which we named Coral Creek, from the many fossil corals among its gravels.... we were glad to come down with our worn-out horses from the snowstorms and rocky slopes of Job's Pass and Coral Creek into the prairie grass along the Saskatchewan, where ponies could trot once more.[18]

Arthur Philemon Coleman (1852-1939)

Arthur Coleman was born to Reverend Francis Coleman and Emmeline Maria Adams at Lachute, Quebec, on April 4, 1852. As his father moved around a great deal, Coleman's early education took place in a number of public schools across Ontario. He then attended Cobourg Collegiate Institute and Victoria College, both in Cobourg, Ontario. In 1876 he received his B.A. from Victoria College and was awarded the Prince of Wales gold medal for academic excellence. He taught three years at the Cobourg Collegiate Institute then obtained his M.A. in geology from Victoria College in 1880. By then Coleman had decided on a career in geology. He obtained his Ph.D. from the University of Breslau in Germany in 1881. It was during his doctoral field studies in various parts of Europe that Coleman developed his love of mountains and life-long interest in alpinism.

When the Canadian Pacific Railway reached Laggan (Lake Louise) in 1884, Coleman was anxious to explore the Canadian Rockies. That year, he travelled to the end of steel at Laggan and proceeded westward as best he could. Over the next 24 years he made eight major exploration trips to the Selkirks and Rockies, establishing his reputation as one of the premier explorers and mountaineers of the time. Mount Coleman, a peak in Banff National Park, was named in his honour in 1902.

In 1906 Coleman eagerly enrolled as one of the founding members of the Alpine Club of Canada (ACC). One of the first objectives of the new club was to climb Mount Robson, the highest mountain in the Canadian Rockies. The membership selected Coleman to execute the task in 1907 and 1908; unfortunately Coleman did not succeed in his task. Nevertheless, in 1910 he was elected to succeed Arthur Wheeler as the second president of the Alpine Club of Canada, a position that he held until 1914. In 1930 he was made an honorary member of the club.

In the meantime, Coleman had been establishing an equally solid reputation in his professional field. He was appointed Professor of Geology and Natural History at Toronto's Victoria College in 1882. When the college became part of the University of Toronto, he became Professor of Geology at the School of Practical Science (1891–1901) then Professor of Geology at the University of Toronto (1901–1922, after which he became Professor Emeritus). During his years at the University of Toronto, Coleman also served as geologist at the Bureau of Mines, Government of Ontario (1893–1909) and dean of the Faculty of Arts (1919–1922). He was appointed director of the Royal Ontario Museum of Geology in Toronto in 1914. After his retirement from the university, he was again employed as a geologist by the Department of Mines, Government of Ontario, between 1931 and 1934.

Over the course of his career, Coleman established a world-wide reputation in the field of geology and received many awards and honours, including election as a Fellow of the Royal Societies of Canada and of England and several honorary degrees. In addition to his work in his chosen field, Coleman was also an accomplished artist, sketching subjects as diverse as geological features, architectural forms, natural wonders, such as waterfalls and mountains, botanical specimens and people. Coleman was modest about his art and refused to commercialize it.

He was also a strong writer, authoring five books and almost two hundred papers and reports over the course of his lifetime. His best-known work, *The Canadian Rockies New and Old Trails*, was first published in 1911. His final work, *The Last Million Years*, published in 1941, was a popular summary of his studies on glaciations. He was in the process of revising the work when he died, unmarried, at home in Toronto on February 26, 1939. Arthur Coleman is still remembered as one of the greatest explorers in the Canadian Rocky Mountains.

Professor A.P. Coleman, one of the greatest explorers in the Canadian Rockies, used Stoney guide Jimmy Jacob's twentieth-century route along the Cline River and over Cataract Pass several times.

Once across the Saskatchewan, the party crossed another divide into the drainage of the Red Deer River and proceeded east and south through the foothills to Morley.[19]

Although the Colemans successfully met the challenge of crossing Job Pass, they did not use the route again. On future trips they instead chose to use the Cline River–Cataract Pass route, which took them to the headwaters of the Brazeau River.[20] No other tourists or adventurers reported using the Job Pass route either until the queen of mountain adventurers, Caroline Hinman, led one of her Off the Beaten Track tours into the region in 1925.[21] They arrived at Coral Creek on July 16 then spent a layover day near Job Pass before proceeding to the Brazeau River and on to Brazeau Lake on July 19.[22]

Hinman liked to follow her long summer outings with an intimate autumn hunting trip. On August 29, 1926 – a mere three days after completing her 55-day summer trip – she, Lillian Gest, Louise Vincent and Hal Learned set out toward Pipestone Pass to hunt.[23] Charlie Hunter outfitted the party, assisted by Bert Mickel, Frank Richter and Jack La Coste. By September 11 they had followed the North Saskatchewan to the mouth of Coral Creek. They then proceeded north along Jacques Cardinal's route, spending the following four days in the vicinity of Job Pass. But a combination of heavy snow and the presence of other hunters in the area pushed them back toward the Kootenay Plains, where they arrived on September 16. They retraced their steps over Pipestone Pass to arrive back in Lake Louise on September 26.[24]

Caroline Hinman was back on part of Jacques Cardinal's old trail the following year, this time with an Off the Beaten Track party of 22. They began at Lake Louise, following David Thompson's old route east along the Red Deer River,[25] then Coleman's route north over Divide Pass to the North Saskatchewan.[26] They proceeded north through the foothills to the Brazeau River and followed Jacques Cardinal's route along the Southesk River. They left the route to visit Southesk Lake, returning just north of Rocky Pass along the Rocky River. Hoping to find a route to Medicine Lake and Jasper, they rejoined Cardinal's trail, which they followed as far as Jacques Lake. Then, instead of following Cardinal's path over Merlin

Pass to the Athabasca, they veered west toward Medicine Lake. They were pleased to discover a good trail around the lake and a wagon road leading along the Maligne River to Jasper.

This moose was having an early morning feed in a flooded area of Breccia Creek, very close to the outlet from Jacques Lake.

DRAMATIC EVENTS

A most unique pack-train trip took place along the south boundary of Jasper National Park in 1930. Led by Mona Harragin, one of the first two licensed female guides in Canada's National Parks, the party spent two weeks travelling the South Boundary Trail from Brazeau Lake to Medicine Lake.[27] Although there was a wrangler to help with the horses, Harragin guided, cooked and helped pack the horses. Later that year, she married a park warden, Charlie Matheson. When Matheson was posted at Maligne Lake in 1935, the Mathesons inadvertently became part of the park's folklore.

Although used only infrequently by tourists and adventurers, today's South Boundary Trail was an important patrol route for wardens keeping watch for poachers and preventing the spread of forest fires. Ed McDonald was the warden responsible for the park's eastern boundary in the late 1920s and early 1930s. Fellow warden Frank Camp reports that in June 1937, McDonald:

> had just left the Grizzly cabin which is the half way shelter between the Rocky and Jacques lake and had travelled about a mile when he surprised a grizzly feeding on buffalo berries (soapolallie). His horse reared, unloaded him and took off. Fortunately the bear also took off leaving Ed on the trail with what later proved to be a broken pelvis. Unable to walk, he crawled on his stomach back to the Grizzly cabin. The accident happened on the edge of the first dry wash west of the cabin and just a short distance away was an old shelter probably used by Ed before the present cabin was built.[28] He made it to this old shelter and if I recall correctly, stayed overnight lying on the ground. His next effort was to make it to the Grizzly cabin.
>
> On his arrival he had great difficulty in getting the door open and once inside even greater difficulty trying to reach the telephone nailed high on the wall. The phone was the old forestry type with the hand crank and separate receiver. His first effort was to knock the receiver off the hook, opening

the transmitter circuit and lying on his back, hollering from a distance hoping someone on the line would hear him. This did not work out so he had to improvise a way of lifting himself up to be able to ring and alert Charlie Matheson, the warden at Maligne Lake. He eventually accomplished this task and a rescue party was sent out from Jasper.[29]

Opposite: Caroline Hinman and Lillian Gest often rounded out their summer season of travels through the Rockies by taking a hunting trip with friends. This group consisted of (l–r) Polly Prescott, Lillian Gest, Marguerite Schneffbacher and Caroline Hinman.

Below: Mona Harragin and her sister, Agnes, were the first female licensed guides in the Canadian National Parks. Mona, shown here loading a pack horse, was widely respected as a tough and independent guide.

The rescue party, led by Warden Frank Wells, built a stretcher and strung it between two horses to transport McDonald to Jasper. It was a long, rough ride. Legend has it that when McDonald recovered and returned to the South Boundary Trail district, he removed the telephone from the wall of the Grizzly Cabin and mounted it close to the floor. Generations of future wardens apparently left the phone in this unusual and inconvenient location in memory of Ed McDonald's ordeal.[30]

Right: Telephones such as these were used widely in backcountry warden cabins in the 1930s. Injured Warden Ed McDonald knocked the receiver off the hook but had difficulty reaching the crank to activate the phone.

Below: This improvised stretcher strung between two horses was used to carry injured warden Ed McDonald back to civilization. (l–r) Alex Wiley, guide Bruce Otto, unknown, Warden Matheson, and unknown. One of the unknown men (likely the one on the right) is Dr. Ross. The other may be Warden Frank Wells.

Opposite: Warden Ed McDonald recovering in hospital after the ordeal of breaking his pelvis while on patrol near the Rocky River.

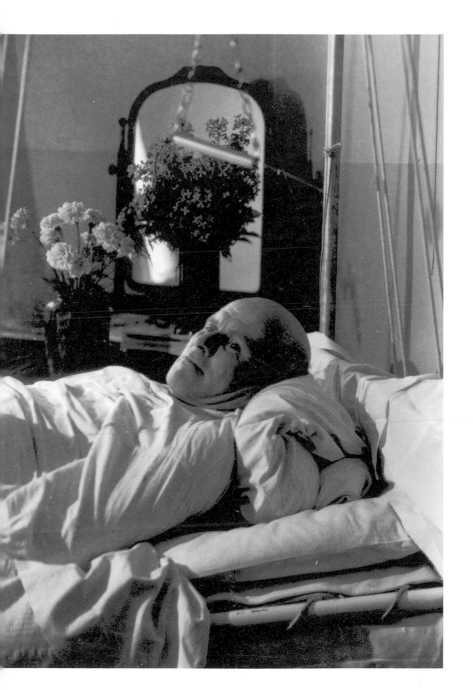

The Trail Today

Today, Jacques Cardinal's route from the Athabasca River to the North Saskatchewan is a long tranquil wilderness hike on which backpackers could easily spend two weeks without seeing anyone. Some stretches are marked by gently undulating countryside that is soothing to the senses, some by rather boring hiking through the forest and others by exceptionally beautiful mountain scenery. Although the entire route is very long, it can be divided into shorter sections, more suitable for most hikers.

The first portion, from the Athabasca River to Jacques Lake, can be hiked by exiting along the Medicine Lake trail from Jacques Lake. Before the road around Medicine Lake was built in the mid-twentieth century, the trail up Jacques Creek and over Jacques and Merlin passes offered the best access to the South Boundary Trail. Now this portion of the trail is seldom used, with most hikers preferring to access Jacques Lake from Medicine Lake.

Most of the trail is uphill, crossing three low passes. The first, Jacques Pass, is particularly scenic. There are many unbridged stream crossings, some requiring fords. Because the trail is not maintained, there are also many fallen trees across it. Rudimentary route-finding skills are required in some places. The trail is suitable for hikers of all ages, provided that they can ford streams and clamber over fallen trees. I did this portion of the Cardinal route as a very long day hike, exiting to Medicine Lake. Most would find the 43 kilometres too long for a single day and would prefer to do this very historic route as a backpacking trip.

The second leg of Cardinal's route, from Jacques Lake to Rocky Pass, can be completed by beginning at Medicine Lake and exiting at the Cardinal Divide. The secret here is to have transportation prearranged, since hitchhiking on the little-used section of secondary road through the Cardinal Divide would be a very chancy proposition. Of course, almost anyone who did happen to be driving that road would likely stop for you.

Much of the first 20 kilometres of the trail from Jacques Lake was totally burned in a large forest fire in 2003. When I hiked the trail the following year, the surface had greened up with lots of grasses and plants, but there was still little evidence of new trees to block the fabulous views the fire opened up. In some areas a massive blow-down would have made the trail virtually impassable, but fortunately a hardworking trail crew had used chainsaws to clear a path through the debris.

I saw many white porcelain insulators on the ground near the trail, evidence of the early telephone line once used by wardens. And an old homemade sheet-metal stove, likely uncovered by the fire, could be seen where an unknown traveller had dropped it by the side of the trail many years ago. The warden cabins and campgrounds along this part of the route also bore evidence of the miracle and devastation of fire. The Grizzly Campground and a small surrounding area had been completely spared, perhaps by a sudden shift in the wind direction. A mere 6 kilometres farther, the Grizzly Warden Cabin and associated outbuilding had been totally destroyed. There is a new cabin on the site, but it rests on a different foundation. The forest fire stopped a short distance beyond the Grizzly Cabin.

This portion of the trail is entirely river-valley hiking, first following Breccia Creek to the Rocky River, then the Rocky and Medicine Tent rivers to the Rocky Pass junction. It does not present any challenges and is suitable for hikers of any age. The forest fire has eliminated (for the time being) any dull forested sections. For those choosing to exit over Rocky Pass, the pass is steep and some minimal route-finding skills are required from the base of the pass to the Cardinal Divide staging area.

The third part of Cardinal's route, over Rocky and Southesk passes to the Brazeau River, retraces the Earl of Southesk's path. Hikers can begin this portion at the Cardinal Divide and exit either along Poboktan Creek (McGillivray's route) or over Nigel Pass. Again, prearranged transportation is highly recommended. The very scenic Rocky Pass is a good way to start this section, followed by some river-valley hiking leading to Southesk Pass, with its views of lakes and mountains and, of course, the historic cairn on the top of the mountain. The approach to the pass and ensuing descent are not steep and make for pleasant hiking.

More river-valley hiking leads to a shock to the senses for most lovers of backcountry wilderness. A short section of this trail lies outside Jasper National Park, and it reveals the devastation that can be caused

Right: The original Grizzly Warden Cabin, which Warden McDonald managed to crawl to with a broken pelvis, was totally destroyed by the 2003 fire. This is its replacement. This photo illustrates how the area to the right was burned out, whereas the forest is still green higher up the mountain side.

Below, left: This old sheet-metal stove, abandoned along the trail many years ago, was no doubt uncovered by the fire.

Below, right: When the wardens installed the single wire telephone lines early in the twentieth century, glass insulators were nailed to trees to support the line. After the 2003 fire, insulators such as these were very evident along the trail, having been freed from their moorings.

Bottom: A large blow-down area between Jacques Lake and the Rocky River would have been extremely difficult travelling before the trail crews cleared the trail after the 2003 forest fire.

by off-highway vehicles in an uncontrolled area. After experiencing the 2.2 kilometres of trail outside the park, most hikers will pause and issue a huge sigh of relief to have returned, perhaps giving silent thanks to the politicians and other leaders of the past century who had the foresight to establish parks to protect some of our wilderness for future generations.

After crossing back into the park, the trail (which had been leading east toward the foothills) does a large hairpin turn to head southwest back into the mountains along the Brazeau River. Shortly after passing a series of shallow ponds, hikers who turn to look back toward the foothills have an exceptional opportunity to clearly see the distinction between the foothills and the mountains. Proceeding down the very beautiful Brazeau River valley, hikers soon reach the spot where Cardinal, Southesk and McGillivray forded the Brazeau River.

In the days of horse travel, crossing the Brazeau River and continuing up the stunning valley of Job Creek was easily accomplished. Today, back-packers would have great difficulty crossing the deep and fast-flowing river; this route is out of the question for all but the hardiest hikers who are also strong swimmers and have a means of getting their packs across. McGillivray did not enter the Job Creek valley but continued east into the foothills. For those wishing to continue on the Cardinal–Southesk route, we provide a hiking guide starting from the south end, as it is not safe for most hikers to ford the Brazeau River at this point. To exit, hikers can follow McGillivray's route along the Brazeau River to Poboktan Creek (Route I above) or continue along the Brazeau River (Route I above) to Nigel Pass (Route III below).

The fourth part of Cardinal's route, the trail north through the Coral and Job creek valleys, is marked by exceptional scenery and numerous creek crossings. This is a horse trail that takes no account of the fact that horses can cross the creek much more easily than humans. There are three choices for travelling along this route. One can leave one's boots on and simply walk through the water as horses do, carrying extra dry footwear for the end of the day. This is not a bad option for a trail with so many fords. The second option is simply to stay on the horse trail, removing one's boots at each ford – a rather time-consuming process. The third option (described in the trail guide) is to bushwhack along the northeast side of Coral Creek at each crossing, picking up the horse trail in ten to 15 minutes. By doing this, only one ford is required. In the Job valley, the bushwhacking option is not viable and the fords are necessary.

Though the Coral Creek valley is very beautiful in its own right, it does not match the majesty of the Job Creek valley. The beauty of the latter, combined with the fact that very few people go there, make it an exceptional destination. Job Pass, high above the treeline, is also a spot of exceptional beauty. Hikers are well-rewarded for their efforts in accomplishing the steep approach and descent.

Most will have to turn around at the Brazeau River and repeat all the fords on the return trip. It may be possible to hike west along the Brazeau River to a point upstream from the outflow of Brazeau Lake (approximately 15 kilometres) and cross the river there, and some maps show a trail along the south side of the Brazeau. I investigated this possibility, and although there did appear to be a trail, it was largely flooded when I was there in mid-July 2005. This route may be feasible later in the summer.

Between the beginning of the hike and the base of Job Pass, the only difficulties encountered are the stream crossings, generally less than knee-deep and not difficult for most adults, although they may present a challenge for younger hikers. The trail is easy to follow and there are many old campsites along the creek. The route over the pass is steep but not otherwise difficult. Near the pass I met up with a father and son fishing duo headed for some unnamed lakes to the west of the route. They had chosen to wade through the fords in their hiking boots and had brought runners to allow for dry feet in camp. Having walked past all the campsites near the creek, they had set up camp in a treeless area near the pass and were very casual about storing their food away from animals, especially bears. They were seasoned travellers and had not experienced problems previously, probably more due to good luck than good planning.

On my return trip, I spotted a black wolf in the Job Creek valley and a grizzly along the side of the trail near the beginning of the Coral Creek trail, and I could not help but think of the two men camped above treeline with their food stored near their tent. Two women on horseback rode up the trail shortly after I spotted the bear. I stopped to chat with them and learned that they were out for a day trip. They were not particularly concerned about the bear but said that they would keep watch so that their horses would not be startled.

As I proceeded down the creek I caught up to the party whose footprints I had been following for some time. It was a group of young teenagers out for several days with a leader, herself an older teen. They had intended to take the Stelfox Pass route, but the entire party of eight had missed the large cairn and flagging tape marking the beginning of the trail and were now returning to the trailhead. I asked them about the bear, since they were ahead of me and would have walked right past it. They were very excited and a bit frightened to think that there was a bear so close to the trail, but none of them had seen it. This group seemed ill-prepared for such an outing and had a very inexperienced leader. Fortunately for them and the two fishermen, Mother Nature can be very forgiving at times.

Steep banks, such as this one, make fording Job Creek a necessity.

Trail Guide

Distances are adapted from existing trail guides: Patton and Robinson, Potter, and Beers, and from Gem Trek maps. Distances intermediate from those given in the sources are estimated from topographical maps and from hiking times. All distances are in kilometres.

From the Athabasca River, along Jacques Creek and over Southesk Pass to the Brazeau River

Maps   Snaring 83 E/1
        Miette 83 F/4
        Medicine Lake 83 C/13
        Mountain Park 83 C/14
        Southesk Lake 83 C/11
        George Creek 83 C/10
        Job Creek 83 C/7
        Jasper and Maligne Lake (Gem Trek)

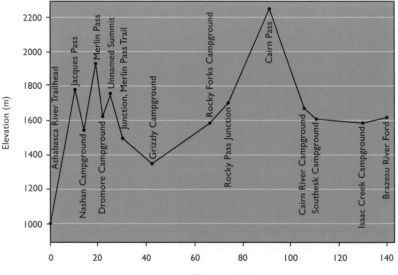

82

Trailhead

The Merlin Pass trailhead is on the right (east) side of the Yellowhead Highway (#16), 20 km north of the Jasper east exit (approximately 3.5 km after crossing the Athabasca River). The trailhead is marked only with a horse–hiker sign. The trail can be reached from the south end by following McGillivray's route (page 44) along the Brazeau River. The section of the trail from the Athabasca River to Jacques Lake is no longer maintained by Parks Canada.

0.0   Trailhead on the east side of Highway 16. A good trail proceeds through a forest of bushes and shrubs to a lake with a beaver dam. The trail skirts the lake and flooded area to the left (north) then follows through thick shrubs along the lake before entering the forest. The trail continues along the left (northeast) side of Jacques Creek, often with good views of the creek, canyon and mountains.

7.3   Cinquefoil Campground. This is a very open spot. Jacques Creek is dry here (July 2005) with a flowing creek coming in from the west. After crossing the flowing creek, the trail continues in a southeasterly direction on the left (northeast) side of (dry) Jacques Creek, which flows underground. The trail is overgrown with shrubs at this point but is still easy to follow. It parallels Jacques Creek, which eventually has water in it. As the trail climbs toward the pass, there are frequent views of the mountains.

10.8   Jacques Pass and Emir Campground. The pass is approached through the trees but at its summit breaks out into an open meadow with good views of the surrounding mountains. The campground is in the trees on the left. There is no visible trail through the meadow, but by continuing southeast to its end, hikers will find a trail at an obvious spot in the trees. The trail drops steadily through a narrow treed valley.

14.8   Nashan Creek Campground. As the trail levels out, it arrives at a small meadow. The campground is off to the right (all signs have been removed). There are three creek crossings in 700 m, all with makeshift bridges (2005). The trail goes straight across a small meadow before entering the forest. It continues uphill, steeply at times, through the forest. Views are limited.

19.2   Merlin Pass, marked with a sign. The top of the pass is heavily treed with no view. The trail then drops downhill through a narrow meadow with good views. Partway along the meadow, the trail enters the woods on the left (northeast) and continues there until reaching another meadow with good views to the left and ahead.

23.3   Dromore Campground. Just beyond the campground is Dromore Creek, which requires two easy fords in the next 15 minutes. The trail again continues uphill through the trees then levels off.

25.5   Unnamed summit. The trail drops steeply downhill through a forest with many deadfalls. It follows a small rushing stream toward Jacques Lake.

29.3   Trail junction and direction signs. The trail intersects the Jacques Lake trail from Medicine Lake (right, or southwest). Turn left (northeast) to continue toward Jacques Lake on the Cardinal–Southesk route. Continue parallel to the lakeshore.

30.3   Jacques Lake Campground. The warden cabin is visible at the northeast end of the lake. After leaving the campground, the trail follows the outlet stream from Jacques Lake (Breccia Creek) past the warden cabin then splits into a hiker (left) and horse (right) trail. For the next 7.4 km, the hiking trail follows Breccia Creek, crossing bridges from one side to the other at least five times. It rejoins the horse trail in about 2 km. Avalanche paths and rock slides provide great views of sheer rock walls as the trail passes through a narrow valley in the Jacques Range.

36.0   The trail enters an area burned by the 2003 forest fire.

37.7   The trail leaves the valley of Breccia Creek and climbs up a steep bank, initially going east along the high ridge then continuing to climb with switchbacks to the southeast, following a ridge high above the Rocky River. It drops to the river flats through a blow-down area.

43.1   Grizzly Campground, on a bank just above the Rocky River in a small area miraculously missed by the fire of 2003. The trail initially climbs high above the river on a bank, and then it drops back down to river level. What would have been heavy forest was completely burned from the 2003 fire, giving great views of the river and mountains.

49.1   Grizzly Warden Cabin. The cabin is new, with the foundations of old cabins still visible where the structures were destroyed by fire. The burned over area ends about 1 km beyond the cabin, though there are some burnt patches farther on. The trail continues along the river, sometimes in deep woods, often through open areas with good views. After passing through a large cleared windfall area the trail splits, with a foot trail going to the right.

51.6   The foot trail becomes a suspension bridge over the Rocky River before it rejoins the horse trail. The trail mostly continues on the river flats, which are quite open with good views of the surrounding mountains.

55.7   Climax Campground. In spite of its name, there is little note-worthy about this campground. The trail continues along the river flats, sometimes in the trees. The river bed has a distinctive sulphur smell.

57.8   Gretna Lake is through the trees on the right (southwest), with no obvious trail to it. The trail skirts the lake on the left side, then continues through the forest.

60.7   Rocky Falls. An opening in the forest gives a good view of the river pounding over the rocks below. The trail continues parallel to the river, sometimes open, sometimes in the forest, often very rocky, with gravelly floodplains from side streams.

66.0   Rocky Forks Campground. Just after the campground, the trail splits, with hikers keeping right to avoid crossing the Medicine Tent River. The trail stays in the woods.

68.0   Trail reaches an open area then rejoins the horse trail. A sign points to the Southesk Lake trail to the right, which follows the Rocky River southward. The sign also points to Rocky Pass, ahead to the southeast. Continue straight ahead as the trail moves in and out of the forest between the floodplain of the Medicine Tent River and a high bank above the river.

71.9   The trail splits again, with hikers keeping to the left on a large gravel floodplain. For the most part, the trail mainly follows close to the river, with great views.

74.9   An old campsite on the river flats. The Medicine Tent Campground is 15 m farther along, right beside the river. Another 15 m ahead is a trail junction, with the trail to Rocky Pass going to the left (north). Continue ahead to the southeast, mainly on the open gravel flats of the river. Pass through a wooden gate across the trail.

79.0   Medicine Tent Warden Cabin. The trail continues to the southeast but in a more southerly direction, mainly in the forest with some open sections.

84.2   Lagrace Campground. The trail continues through open forest and along the edges of meadows, generally with good views on both sides. The trail gradually gets steeper, rockier and more open.

88.6   An open meadow with three small lakes: the Medicine Tent Lakes. The trail continues moderately uphill over very open terrain, mainly above treeline, with fabulous views of the mountains and lakes. On a clear day, Southesk's cairn is visible on top of the mountain to the left.

92.2   A sign reads, "Cairn Pass, 2250 m." The descent is much like the ascent, very open and scenic.

94.2   Cairn Pass Campground. This is a large camp for both hikers and equestrians. The trail continues along the side of a bush-covered meadow, with brief forays into the forest.

97.2   The Cairn River Warden Cabin is clearly visible on the southwest side of the river, with a footbridge across the river leading to the cabin. The trail drops down to the river, and another trail leads back to the warden cabin. The trail is quite open, mainly following the bank of the Cairn River.

104.3   Ford of the Cairn River, relatively easy. Continue along the left (south) side of the river; climb over a ridge.

106.7   Junction. The trail from Southesk Lake comes in from the right (southwest) and joins the main trail, which is now heading east. Shortly after this junction is another ford of the Cairn River, followed by the Cairn River Campground immediately across the river. From the campground the trail follows a straight line through the woods, returning close to the river in a deep ravine. The trail drops down to the river, where yellow markers indicate a horse ford. The hiking trail stays on the left (north) side of the river, and a sign indicates a footbridge and hiking trail.

111.1   Park Boundary. A well-used trail continues through the woods bearing left (northeast) along a seismic line. Although this area is outside the park, there are still Parks Canada signs directing hikers back into the park. The signs direct hikers first to the right, then to the left, then to the right again. The trail is now a quad (off-highway vehicle) road and is an excellent example of the desecration caused by these vehicles. The trail along the muddy quad road is marked by blazes, then a national park sign appears as a beacon, directing hikers down into a steep ravine toward the Southesk River.

113.3   Suspension bridge across the river and national park boundary. The trail climbs to the top of the ravine and joins the horse trail.

114.0   Trail junction. A sign points left (north) on a heavily used horse trail to the Southesk River and on to the Cardinal River farther north. Continue to the right (southeast).

115.6   Southesk Campground. From the campground, the trail heads straight southeast through the forest.

115.9   Junction. A trail sign points straight ahead to Dowling Ford, which is on the Brazeau River and leads out of the park. Follow the sign that points to the right (south) toward Isaac Creek. The trail continues through a meadow-like area. Ahead is a large gap between two mountains. This is where the Brazeau River exits the Front Ranges. The trail passes a series of shallow ponds on the left (east), with high mountains to the right (west): a very beautiful spot.

121.4   A large meadow on the left (east), very open. Continue parallel to the river, through an exceptionally scenic open area.

128.1   Isaac Creek ford. Just across this broad, rapidly flowing creek is the Isaac Creek Campground, which is for both hikers and equestrians.

129.4   Junction. Isaac Creek Warden Cabin is a short distance to the left. Trail continues to the right (south).

130.6   The trail splits again, with a trail to the left leading to the cabin. The main trail continues through the forest parallel to the river, with occasional riverbank viewpoints offering good views of the valley.

135.9   Trail splits: the horse trail goes to the left (east) while the hiking trail goes to the right (west) to avoid a large pond and wetland.

137.8   Hiking trail rejoins the horse trail.

139.2   After passing the large mountain across the river to the right, Job Creek's gap is visible between the mountains.

139.3   A circular pond in the woods on the right. The trail drops down toward the river, passes a meadow on the left and continues through the woods. Somewhere along this stretch the trail turns from a southeast direction to a southwest direction. At about this point, both the Cardinal and Southesk parties would have headed east, forded the Brazeau River and followed Job Creek to the southeast. This is the end of this portion of the Cardinal–Southesk trail. Hikers who have the ability to ford deep fast-flowing rivers can ford the Brazeau here and continue on the Job Creek trail (see below). Most hikers will want to exit along the McGillivray route by following the Brazeau River upstream (southwest) (see Route 1 above).

141.0   Arête Warden Cabin, kilometre 52.0 on the McGillivray route (Route 1 above).

141.8   Arête Campground, kilometre 51.2 on the McGillivray route (Route 1 above).

From Medicine Lake to Merlin Pass Junction

Maps   83 C/13 Medicine Lake

Jasper and Maligne Lake (Gem Trek)

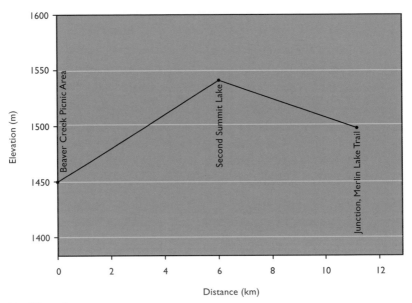

Trailhead

Follow Highway 16 east from Jasper and turn right on the Maligne Road, following it to the southeast end of Medicine Lake (28 km). The trailhead is at the Beaver Creek Picnic Area, on the left (north) side of the road.

0.0   Beaver Creek Picnic Area. The trail starts out as a hard-packed gravel road. Within minutes, it reaches a warden cabin. Continue up the road with Beaver Creek on the right (east).

1.6   Beaver Lake. There is a dock with boats and canoes at the south end. A major picnic area with tables is situated along the lakeshore. At the end of the lake are the remains of an old campsite, with a stone and mortar fire pit. The road continues along this scenic valley.

4.8 First Summit Lake. The trail skirts the lake to the right (east) and becomes a single-track hiking, biking and horse trail.

6.0 Second Summit Lake. The trail skirts this lake on the right (east). Beyond the end of the lake is a meadow with another small shallow lake and good views of the surrounding mountains. The trail swings to the northeast and continues along Beaver Creek.

11.2 Junction. Merlin Pass trail goes to the left. This is kilometre 29.3 of the Jacques Creek to Brazeau Lake trail above.

Beautiful Jacques Lake, named after Jacques Cardinal, is on the South Boundary Trail circuit, which begins at Medicine Lake. Jacques Lake is just beyond the junction with the Merlin Pass trail. It is most often visited by day hikers, but this view of early morning mist on the lake is only available to those who spend a night on its shores.

From the Medicine Tent River to the Cardinal Divide

Map   83 C/14 Mountain Park

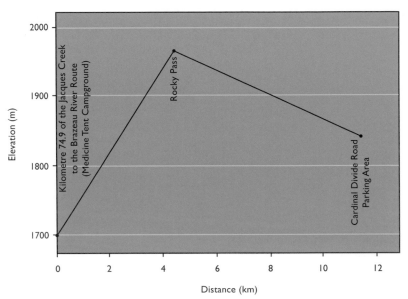

Trailhead

For those hiking the Cardinal–Southesk route from the Athabasca River to the Brazeau, the trailhead is kilometre 74.9 on that route (see trail guide above), 100 m south of the Medicine Tent Campground. From the east, the trailhead can be accessed by taking Highway 40 from Hinton south to its junction with the Cadomin road (48 km). Turn right through the village of Cadomin and continue along this narrow, rough and winding road to the Cardinal Divide (23 km), which is clearly marked with signs and a large parking area. Continue another 1.7 km to the trailhead, which has a large parking area and space for overnight camping.

0.0   From the trail junction (kilometre 74.9) on the Cardinal–Southesk route, the trail climbs steadily through the trees with a moderate grade then continues to climb along a rocky and barren ravine with several good viewpoints.

2.5 Viewpoint marked by a cairn on top of a ridge. This is likely the high point of the trail. It gives a good view over the broad, flat, treeless pass ahead. From the top of this ridge, the trail drops gently, crosses a rocky alluvial fan followed by a dry creek bed and enters the grassy flats of the pass.

4.4 National park boundary and the top of the pass. There is a brass survey marker here, a small lake to the left (west) and two dominant mountains on either side of the pass: Mount Cardinal to the west and Mount McKenzie to the east.

4.7 Another cairn marking the summit of the pass. From here the trail heads downhill.

5.7 End of the open pass area. The trail drops straight down through the trees. It is very rough, rocky, rooty and wet.

7.0 First of three knee-deep fords of the Cardinal River in less than I km. The trail climbs the riverbank, offering good views of the river and the pass.

9.7 Outfitter's camp. From here the trail largely follows the edge of meadows, which feature several small ponds. There is a cut line along the left side of the meadow. Hikers can either cross over to the cut line or follow the horse trail on the right side of the meadow. The horse trail and the cut line eventually join.

I I.4 Parking area and trailhead.

From the North Saskatchewan River over Job Pass to the Brazeau River

Distances for this trail only are estimated from topographical maps and hiking times. All distances are in kilometres.

Maps   83 C/1 Whiterabbit Creek
        83 C/2 Cline River
        83 C/7 Job Creek
        Alberta's Bighorn Wildland Recreation Area brochure, Alberta Forestry, Lands and Wildlife.

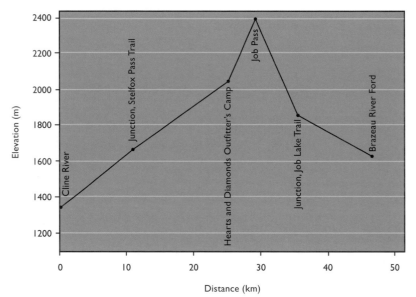

Trailhead

This trail begins at the Cline River trailhead on the David Thompson Highway (#11), 4 km south of the David Thompson Resort. The large parking area is on the left (west) side of the highway, just north of the Cline River bridge and is clearly marked with a large sign, which reads: "Cline River/Coral Creek Staging Area." The north end of the trail is at approximately kilometre 139 of the Cardinal–Southesk route (see above) and requires a major ford of the Brazeau River, which is not recommended for hikers. Most will have to retrace their steps back to the trailhead. This trail is entirely within the Bighorn Wildland Recreation Area.

0.0   Cline River–Coral Staging Area. A well-beaten horse trail leads uphill parallel to Coral Creek and continues uphill along the very scenic Coral Creek Canyon. The trail then drops sharply down to creek level.

3.1   Trail junction. The trail along the Cline River fords Coral Creek and continues to the west. Do not cross the creek; continue ahead (northwest) up Coral Creek on a heavily used horse trail. There are many old campsites along the creek in this area. The horse trail crosses the creek twice in the next kilometre. The fords can be avoided by taking a faint trail along the right (northeast) bank of the creek, which rejoins the horse trail in a short distance.

4.3   Immediately after rejoining the horse trail for the second time, there is an old outfitter's camp beside the creek. A similar one is found 1.4 km farther along the trail. Hikers soon reach another ford, which can easily be avoided by staying on the right side. The next ford can also be avoided by keeping to the right of a side stream of the main creek. You will see two old campsites shortly after you rejoin the horse trail.

8.9   The trail drops to creek level and fords the creek. This time the right (east) bank is too steep to avoid the ford. It is best to follow the right bank to the sheer rock face then ford the creek to the left and immediately ford the creek again to the right (northeast) just upstream from the rock face, effectively having to ford only once. The next ford can easily be avoided by keeping on the right side, as before. When you rejoin the horse trail you will see two more campsites. The trail now enters the forest.

11.2   A rock cairn and flagging tape mark the junction with the trail going to the right (northeast) over Stelfox Pass. Continue ahead (northwest) up the creek valley, generally along creek level but occasionally high above the creek. There are two more fords that can be avoided by keeping to the right of the creek and two more old campsites in the next 3.6 km. The valley is very scenic, with occasional dramatic views of the mountains.

14.8   An old campsite beside the creek contains the remains of a tiny cabin or food cache. Continue along the creek past another old campsite and another ford, which can be avoided, again by keeping to the right.

19.8   Old outfitter's camp. Shortly thereafter, cross a large dry creek bed to a large meadow covered in bushes. The trail continues away from the creek on the right (northwest) then splits, with the left branch leading to an outfitter's camp on the meadow. Continue ahead along the creek past the end of the meadow, with great views of fabulous mountains all around.

25.0   Hearts and Diamonds Outfitter's Camp. This is a very large campground that straddles the creek. From the portion north of the creek, a trail leads southwest to the headwaters of Coral Creek. Take the trail from the first campsite, which leads right (east) into heavy forest and begins the climb toward Job Pass. The trees become progressively smaller, with occasional viewpoints into a steep-walled canyon. The well-used trail crosses a meadow then begins the steep climb through a very open area toward the pass.

29.3   Top of Job Pass. This is a very beautiful area and a worthwhile destination in itself. From the top of the pass, the trail drops steeply through an open area that becomes more treed as it nears a willow-covered meadow in the Job Creek valley. The trail continues across the very beautiful meadow and passes an old campsite, where the trail stays to the right (northeast) of Job Creek.

32.7   Large outfitter's camp just across a small creek. The trail soon reaches the first ford (calf-deep) of Job Creek.

34.3   Forested area at the end of the long and glorious meadow. Ford Job Creek then continue along through this meadow-like area. Three more fords of Job Creek follow, the third being very close to the second. This is an exceptionally beautiful valley.

36.0   The trail splits with a branch to the left (southwest) going to Job Lake. Continue ahead (northwest). There is a large outfitter's camp at the junction. Continue along the open valley.

37.0   Junction. The trail to the right (northeast) goes to an outfitter's camp on the side of the meadow. Continue ahead down the valley; ford Job Creek three more times. The trail then enters a narrow ravine and climbs to its top.

43.1   A major trail comes in along a cut line from the left (southwest). Continue climbing to the northwest until the trail turns north along a cut line and begins its descent. The trail follows a heavily used horse trail, first heading northwest then west, continually changing direction.

46.5   The trail reaches the extensive gravel flats of Whisker Creek and an outfitter's camp. Continue along the creek's bank without crossing it.

47.0   Brazeau River. The river is fast, wide and deep. Horse traffic can ford the river along this area. Hikers are advised to turn back.

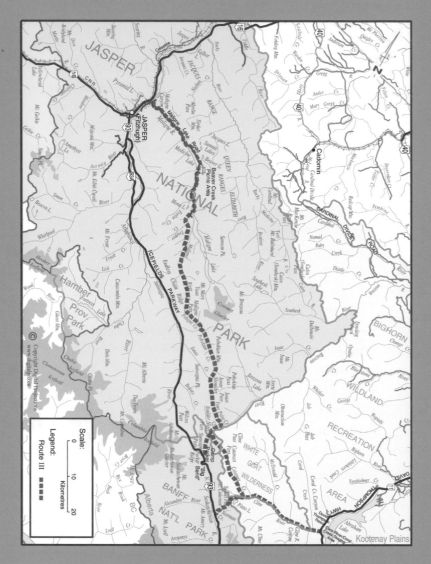

Old Klyne's Trail from the Athabasca River to the North Saskatchewan River via the Maligne and Cline rivers.

ROUTE III

Chaba Imne: Old Klyne's Trail from the Athabasca to the North Saskatchewan Rivers via the Maligne and Cline Rivers (including Nigel and Sunset Passes)

Although I hiked all the trails in the *Life of the Trail* series in order to get up-to-date trail information, I did not follow any particular sequence. Often, I combined parts of different hikes for the sake of convenience. In this case, I hiked an eight-day loop from Medicine Lake along the Cardinal–Southesk route (Route II above), followed by McGillivray's route (Route I above) and a portion of Old Klyne's Trail to Maligne Lake. Because the distance between the two lakes by road is considerable, I planned to hitch a ride. Feeling that it was unfair to ask a stranger to pick up and transport someone who had been on the trail for eight days, I decided to leave my van at the Maligne Lake parking lot and hitch a ride to the start of the hike.

Just as I was parking my van, a rented motorhome was pulling out from a parking space immediately behind me. A woman was standing behind the large vehicle, directing the driver in the crowded parking lot. This seemed like too good an opportunity to miss. I immediately went over to her, explained my situation and asked if I could get a ride as far as Medicine Lake. She did not seem to know where the lake was but readily agreed to take me.

Once we were underway, I realized that the woman I had first spoken with was the only person in the vehicle speaking English. The family was from Germany and were vacationing in the Rockies. I asked my confrere what she did for a living and she replied that she taught English back in Germany. We had a lively conversation on the drive to the lake, with her translating for other members of the family. She often tripped up in figures of speech with which she was unfamiliar but very anxious to learn. I considered myself very lucky to have gotten a ride so easily – not to mention with such a friendly and interesting family.

The beauty of Maligne Lake has been amazing visitors since Michael Klyne first visited its shores 1824. In the early twentieth century, Mary Schäffer was instrumental to the lake's protection within Jasper National Park.

CHRONOLOGY

1824 Michael Klyne, the Hudson's Bay Company factor at Jasper House, has a special trail cut up the Maligne River to Maligne Lake, over Maligne and Jonas passes to Cataract Pass and down the Cline River to the Kootenay Plains.

1875 Surveyor Henry McLeod becomes the first recorded non-Native visitor to travel to Maligne Lake along part of Old Klyne's Trail as he searches out a possible route for the Canadian Pacific Railway.

1892 Lucius Coleman and Stoney guide Jimmy Jacob are the first travellers to record using the southern end of Old Klyne's Trail (which runs from Poboktan Creek over Jonas Shoulder and Pass to the Brazeau River, then over Cataract Pass and down Cataract Creek to the Cline River and the Kootenay Plains).

1893 The Coleman brothers, accompanied by Professor Stewart and young Morley rancher Frank Sibbald, travel from the Kootenay Plains along the Coleman–Jacob route over Cataract Pass to the headwaters of the Brazeau River. They continue over a new pass (later named Jonas Pass), which leads to the Sunwapta River.

   When the Colemans first arrive at Pinto Lake, they climb to the top of the ridge overlooking the lake, gaining a view into the valley of the North Saskatchewan. This is the first report of anyone crossing today's Sunset Pass, called Pinto Pass by early travellers.

1898 Hugh Stutfield and Bill Peyto make the first recorded crossing of Nigel Pass.

1902 The Colemans again use the Cataract Pass–Cline River portion of Old Klyne's Trail.

1906 Returning from the Columbia Icefield to the Kootenay Plains, Mary Schäffer, Mollie Adams, Billy Warren and Sid Unwin cross Pinto (Sunset) Pass to Pinto Lake then follow Klyne's trail down the Cline River.

1907   Mary Schäffer and her party explore north from the base of Cataract Pass, following Old Klyne's Trail over Jonas Pass. They return to their camp and cross Cataract Pass in several feet of snow to reach Pinto Lake. The men proceed to cross Pinto (Sunset) Pass to obtain food from a cache on the North Saskatchewan River before continuing over well-worn Stoney trails along the Cline River to the Kootenay Plains.

1908   Mary Schäffer and her companions cross Nigel Pass again at the beginning of the trip, leading to their discovery of Maligne Lake. They reach Maligne Lake (*Chaba Imne*) from the south then attempt to follow the Maligne River to Jasper but are thwarted by an abundance of fallen timber.

1909   On an epic journey from Lacombe, Alberta, to British Columbia's Fraser River, a group reluctantly uses Nigel Pass to exit the Brazeau drainage. The party consists of guide Fred Stephens; a civil engineer named Sawyer; Fred's brother, Nick, as packer; a cook called Tom; and the client, Stanley Washburn.

1910   Jimmy Simpson, packer Ernie Brearley and artist Carl Rungius travel together as far as Wilcox Pass then retreat to Nigel Pass and Jonas Pass.

1911   Rungius returns to the Nigel Pass–Jonas Pass area with fellow artist Philip Goodwin.

Curly Phillips leads climber Reverend George Kinney, photographer Byron Harmon and Swiss guide Conrad Kain south over Maligne Pass from Maligne Lake. They reach Lake Louise in a record 12 days. In early October, Phillips and Kain return north. The round trip is the first known to be accomplished in less than a month.

1912   Jack Brewster leads a pack train from Lake Louise to Jasper along the Bow and Sunwapta rivers to Poboktan Creek then east along the McGillivray–Coleman route on Poboktan Creek. Brewster manages to locate the creek leading north to Maligne Pass.

1914   Sid Unwin rediscovers the trail connecting Jonas Creek to the Poboktan Creek trail via Jonas Shoulder.

Fred Brewster and Phil Moore cut a trail from the Athabasca River to the old Native trail leading from Jacques Lake to the southeast end of Medicine Lake.

Jimmy Simpson leads Mrs. Crandell and Mrs. Chandler of Philadelphia along Mary Schäffer's route to Maligne Lake. On their return to the Kootenay Plains, they visit Pinto Lake and travel down the Cline River.

1915   Jimmy Simpson leads a group of New Yorkers over Nigel Pass, Jonas Pass, Jonas Shoulder and Poboktan Pass to the Brazeau Lake valley, where they spend two weeks hunting and enjoying camp life.

1916   Simpson takes another pair of hunters, Robert Frothingham and George Martin, to the Brazeau River country over Nigel Pass. This time they set up camp on Cataract Creek.

1918   The trail up the east side of the Maligne River is completed to Maligne Lake and the trail up the Maligne River to Medicine Lake is upgraded to the status of wagon road.

1920s   Jasper outfitter Fred Brewster's saddle-horse trips from Jasper to Maligne Lake and back over Shovel Pass include following the new wagon road from the end of Medicine Lake to Maligne Lake. Gaining employment guiding these trips allows the Harragin sisters, Agnes and Mona, to become the first female licensed trail guides in Canada's national parks.

1923   Jasper outfitter Jack Brewster initiates his three-week Glacier Trail pack-train trip from Jasper to Lake Louise and back. He begins by following the trail to Maligne Lake then continues over Maligne and Jonas passes to Nigel Pass.

Caroline Hinman leads a pack train of 23 pack horses and 17 saddle horses along the route to Maligne Lake with the assistance of guide Curly Phillips; helpers Ed Neighbour, David and Frank Moberly, and Lewis Swift; and Jack Jensen, the cook.

1924   Mountain photographer Byron Harmon and writer Lewis Freeman ask Soapy Smith, Rob Baptie and Ulysses La Casse to assist with a circular pack-train trip from Lake Louise to Jasper and back. They return along Old Klyne's Trail from Jasper to the Kootenay Plains.

Group of Seven artists Lawren Harris and A.Y. Jackson arrive in Jasper, intending to paint for the Canadian National Railway. They walk to Maligne Lake and set up camp.

Caroline Hinman's Off the Beaten Track tour essentially repeats Mary Schäffer's trip of 1906. While at Pinto Lake, the group takes a side trip to Cataract Pass before continuing down the Cline River.

1925   Jimmy Simpson leads a party of three Philadelphia businessmen from Nigel Pass over Jonas and Maligne passes and down the Maligne River to Jasper.

1927   Caroline Hinman uses the trail to Maligne Lake on another of her Off the Beaten Track tours.

1928   One of Hinman's tours meets up with another group at Medicine Lake and escorts them along Old Klyne's Trail over Maligne, Jonas and Cataract passes to Pinto Lake. They then leave Klyne's route to travel west over Sunset Pass.

1930   A one-way auto road is completed from Jasper to the north end of Medicine Lake and a boat service established to transport tourists to the south end of the lake. From there, they travel to Maligne Lake by pack train.

1933   On a horseback trip from southern Alberta to the Pacific Ocean, Cliff and Ruth Kopas cross Nigel Pass and follow the Brazeau River to Brazeau Lake.

1940   Tourists can now drive to Medicine Lake, put their car on a ferry to cross the lake then drive to Maligne Lake, all in only three hours.

1969   Plans are afoot to build a road from Maligne Lake to the Icefields Parkway over Maligne Pass. The first step is to build a highway bridge over the Maligne River at Maligne Lake. Fortunately, this is as far as the project proceeds due to negative public reaction.

Early travellers reached Maligne Lake from the south by crossing Nigel Pass, following the Brazeau River to Brazeau Lake and then heading west toward Poboktan Pass. Most would have caught this view of Brazeau Lake, taken from the trail to the John-John Creek valley. Brazeau, one of the largest backcountry lakes, is set off by the glacier-covered peaks of Le Grand Brazeau Range in the background.

History

Klyne's Entire Route

At the end of the summer of 1858, the Palliser Expedition's James Hector travelled along the Bow–Mistaya corridor to the North Saskatchewan. After exploring in the Howse Pass region, he proceeded to follow the Saskatchewan east to the Kootenay Plains, en route to Fort Edmonton.[1] His Stoney guide, Nimrod, remarked that there was a trail running from the Kootenay Plains all the way to the Athabasca River. This trail, known today as Old Klyne's Trail, follows the Cline River valley.

The trail was named for Michael Klyne, a fur trader who joined the North West Company in about 1798 and remained with the Hudson's Bay Company (HBC) after the two companies amalgamated in 1821. From 1824 until his 1835 retirement, Klyne was responsible for the company's post at Jasper House. Tension between the eastern Kootenay and Shuswap bands and the Blackfoot Confederacy pushed Klyne and his men to travel east to trade with the former. To facilitate the journey, he had a trail cut up the Maligne River to Maligne Lake, over Maligne and Jonas passes to Cataract Pass then down today's Cline River to the Kootenay Plains. These annual trade meetings, which continued with various HBC factors until the early 1870s, led to the naming of the Kootenay Plains.[2] In 1902 mountaineer Norman Collie named the Cline River in Michael Klyne's honour.[3]

There is no reported use of Old Klyne's Trail between the end of the fur trade and the early twentieth century. Even during the fourth period of exploration, that of the tourist-explorers and mountaineers, very few parties used the entire trail – although there are many reports of groups using various portions of it.[4] In 1924 famed mountain photographer Byron Harmon decided to take a circular pack-train trip from Lake Louise to

Byron Harmon is the most celebrated photographer of the Canadian Rockies. In 1924 he and his friend, Lewis Freeman, completed a trip from Lake Louise to Jasper and back so Harmon could add to his extensive collection of mountain photographs. The last part of the route was along Old Klyne's Trail.

Above: Lewis Freeman accompanied his friend Byron Harmon on a trip from Lake Louise to Jasper and back. Freeman was a travel writer and took the opportunity to collect material for his book, *On the Roof of the Rockies*.

Opposite: Ptarmigan on Jonas Shoulder after an early-season snowfall. Harmon and Freeman encountered much more snow on their 1924 trip.

Jasper and back in order to round out his portfolio of Rocky Mountain photographs. Accompanying him were his friend, writer Lewis Freeman, head guide Soapy Smith, wrangler Rob Baptie and cook Ulysses La Casse.[5] They left on August 15 with 16 horses and two dogs.

They began by following the Bow and Mistaya rivers to the Saskatchewan then crossing to the drainage of the Sunwapta and following it and the Athabasca to Jasper.[6] The party left Jasper on October 2 to return to Banff. Although there is no indication that any of them had heard of Klyne or his travels, they found an easy-to-follow trail up the Maligne River from the Athabasca to Medicine Lake, around the lake and on to Maligne Lake.[7]

They stopped to photograph the spectacular lake and rest the horses, then they departed for Maligne Pass on the morning of October 7 – only to find it buried beneath two feet of snow. Undaunted, they continued on to Poboktan Creek. Harmon wanted to shoot what he called his "snow picture:" a photograph of a pack train travelling through a landscape that was nothing but snow. In a decision that inadvertently kept the party on Old Klyne's Trail, Harmon determined that his best chance lay in guiding the pack train up Poboktan Creek and over Jonas Shoulder and Pass. He was not disappointed. Snow was heavy on the high passes and La Casse had to walk ahead, leading his horse, in order to break trail. Such was the cost of fulfilling Harmon's artistic ambitions.

Fortunately, travel became much easier as they descended into the broad open valley of Four Point Creek and on into the Brazeau River valley. They encountered more heavy snow in the high pass between the Brazeau and Cataract Creek, but the lower elevation of the creek did not present any difficulty as they proceeded on to Pinto Lake, just west of the junction of Cataract Creek with the Cline River. They continued down the Cline River to the Kootenay Plains, thus completing Klyne's route. From there, Harmon and Freeman continued south along Whiterabbit Creek to the Clearwater River, which they followed downstream into the foothills.[8]

The following year, 1925, Jimmy Simpson led a group of three Philadelphian businessmen, H.E. Sibson, Samuel Felix and E.S. Higgins, along part of Klyne's trail from the Brazeau River to Jasper Park Lodge (near the Athabasca River).[9] They entered the Brazeau country by crossing Nigel Pass, where they joined Klyne's route over Jonas and Maligne passes to Maligne Lake. After a layover at Maligne Lake, the party continued down the Maligne River past Medicine Lake and on to Jasper.

Three years later, Caroline Hinman completed her summer of touring in the mountains by following Old Klyne's Trail from the Athabasca River to Pinto Lake. She had just completed a trip along the South Boundary Trail, ending at Medicine Lake.[10] At this point, some of the travellers returned to Jasper and several new ones joined the group. The combined group continued over Maligne Pass to Poboktan Creek. They spent two days resting near Poboktan Pass then headed south over Jonas Shoulder and Pass. They reached the Brazeau River on August 9, proceeded to its headwaters, crossed Cataract Pass and followed Cataract Creek downstream to Pinto Lake. This marked the end of that summer's travels on Old Klyne's Trail. Hinman's party proceeded to cross Pinto Pass (Sunset Pass) on August 13 and continued down the Saskatchewan River valley.

Opposite above: Pinto Lake, taken from near the top of Sunset Pass looking northeast.

Opposite below: The Cline River valley, looking east, from partway down the Sunset Pass trail. Pinto Lake can be seen on the right.

McLeod's Maligne River Section

The paved road from the Athabasca River to Medicine Lake, around the north side of the lake and on to Maligne Lake was not built until well into the twentieth century. Previously, travel to Maligne Lake had often been a very tortuous undertaking. But the tough terrain deterred neither the Stoneys from the south nor the Moberly family and other Métis hunters and trappers from the north, all of whom frequently travelled through the area surrounding the lake.[11]

The first recorded non-Native to visit Maligne Lake was surveyor H.A.F. McLeod.[12] McLeod spent the summer of 1875 seeking out a possible route for the Canadian Pacific Railway between the Saskatchewan and Athabasca rivers. On September 8, he followed the Maligne River to Maligne Lake, noting Maligne Canyon and the underground outlet of Medicine Lake en route. Apparently rather weary upon reaching the lake, McLeod named it Sorefoot Lake and, having realized that the route up the Maligne River was not suitable for a railway, continued on his way without giving the area a second thought. He proceeded east to the Rocky River and descended it to its mouth at the Athabasca – only to determine that it, too, was unsuitable for a railway.

Although McLeod apparently had little difficulty reaching Maligne Lake by following the Maligne River, the reverse trip proved to be impossible for a 1908 party. Mary Schäffer and her companions reached Maligne Lake from the south in early July of that year.[13] In spite of the considerable difficulty posed by the large undertow at this point, they managed to cross the Maligne River near its source at the lake, intending to follow it to Fitzhugh (Jasper). Much to their dismay, they found that a large amount of fallen timber had rendered the trail along the river virtually impassable for horses. After several days of cutting, the guides were forced to concede defeat. The party retraced their steps across the Maligne River and over Maligne Pass to Poboktan Creek, from whence they followed Coleman's trail along the creek to the Sunwapta River.[14] They then proceeded north along the Athabasca to the Miette River and Yellowhead Pass.

By 1912 outfitters – most notably the Brewsters, the Ottos and Curly Phillips – had set up businesses in Fitzhugh. Two years later, Fred Brewster

Outfitter Fred Brewster, who had established
his business in Fitzhugh (Jasper) in 1912, was
awarded the contract to cut a trail up the
Maligne River as far as Medicine Lake in 1914.
This photo shows him lighting his pipe with a
burning stick from a campfire.

and partner Phil Moore were awarded a contract to cut a trail from the Athabasca River to the old Native trail leading from Jacques Lake to the southeast end of Medicine Lake. From there, anyone proceeding to Maligne Lake could follow a Native trail across the Maligne River (where it flowed into Medicine Lake) then travel south through open country toward the old entrance to Shovel Pass in the Evelyn Creek valley. The trail then followed Evelyn Creek to the Maligne River and the Maligne to Maligne Lake.[15]

Early travellers spent three days following this trail from Jasper to Maligne Lake. As trail conditions improved, the route could be completed in only two days, and by 1918, the trail up the east side of the Maligne River had been extended to the lake, providing travellers with a considerably shorter route. The trail up the Maligne River to Medicine Lake was also upgraded to the status of a wagon road.

In the late 1920s, the saddle-horse trip from the end of Medicine Lake to Maligne Lake became part of a circle trip from Jasper to Maligne Lake and back over Shovel Pass run by Jasper outfitter Fred Brewster.[16] In 1927 Brewster hired sisters Agnes and Mona Harragin to operate his tent camp at the south end of Medicine Lake. The following year, they were hired as trail guides for the circle trip, becoming the first female licensed trail guides in Canada's national parks.[17] As might be expected, these hardworking and conscientious sisters were very popular with the tourists, especially around Jasper, where most of the circle trips ended. Mona Lake, near the south end of the Shovel Pass trail, is named after the tough and self-reliant Mona Harragin.

In 1914, the year Fred Brewster and Phil Moore first cut the trail to Medicine Lake, only three visitors made the trip. By 1927 the number of annual visitors to Maligne Lake had increased to 130; ten years later, more than five hundred made the trip. The number of people wanting to visit Maligne Lake, one of the most spectacular destinations in the Jasper area, soon outgrew the outfitters' ability to transport them from the end of Medicine Lake by horseback.

By 1930 a one-way auto road had been completed as far as the north end of Medicine Lake and a boat service established to transport tourists

Mona (1904–1983) and Agnes (1906–1988) Harragin

Canada's first female licensed trail guides in the national parks – Mona and Agnes Harragin – were born in Port of Spain, Trinidad, on November 20, 1904, and March 4, 1906, respectively. Although both of their parents were born in the West Indies, the family moved to a small farm near Salmon Arm, BC, when Agnes was only two years old. There the girls developed a love of the outdoors and inherited their father's fondness for horses. Because they had fine equestrian skills, a friend suggested they might find employment guiding in the national parks. Inquiries to both Jasper and Banff national parks resulted in the same answer: outfitters did not hire women as guides. But Jasper's Fred Brewster did need women to assist at his tent camps, and the Harragin sisters jumped at the opportunity. They arrived in Jasper in June of 1927.

Their first charge was the Medicine Lake tent camp, where tourists commonly stopped for lunch on their way to Maligne Lake and occasionally stayed overnight. Working at the camp provided them with an opportunity to meet many people, learn the workings of the tourist business and – most important – get to know the surrounding area intimately. The outfitters, guides and wardens who passed through were only too happy to share their insights about the outfitting business, and the young women helped out by wrangling horses for the men who stayed overnight.

Although their summer was very successful, the sisters turned down Fred Brewster's offer of similar camp employment for the following summer. Determined to work as guides, they requested a job working with horses. Finally Brewster offered them work as guides on the circle trip from Jasper Park Lodge to Maligne Lake and back. The Harragins were overjoyed with the offer, which they later discovered to have been a result of Mrs. Brewster putting her foot down and insisting that the sisters deserved a chance. As a result, Parks Canada issued guide licenses to both women in 1928.

Though Mona and Agnes shared a string of 35 horses, the sisters worked independently. The men who were hired to wrangle and pack for them that summer did not show up, and the men in the Brewster barn gave them slow or poorly trained horses. But the women never complained. They worked with the horses they were given and did all the wrangling, packing and tying of the famous diamond hitch themselves. Over the course of the summer, they proved themselves to be very competent guides. And, as might be expected, were also very popular with the tourists; the Stetsons, monogrammed chaps and colourful scarves they wore made them very photogenic.

As a result of the severe Depression, the Harragins were let go early in the 1930 season. They accepted part-time employment with another Jasper outfitter, Hughes and Kitchen, mainly leading day trips around town. Mona also guided two long trips that year: one to the Tonquin Valley and another to Brazeau Lake.

On October 6, 1930, Agnes married Mark Truxler, who had worked as a packer for Brewster. Two months later, on New Year's Eve, Mona married Warden Charlie Matheson. The Truxlers moved to Entrance, Alberta, (just outside the park) in 1936, where Mark worked at various ranch and outfitter jobs until he joined Parks Canada, retiring in 1970. The Truxlers had two children, Vernon Harragin Truxler (born in 1931) and Jacqueline Mona Truxler (born in 1934).[18] After Mark's retirement, they moved to a small ranch near Hinton. Agnes died on August 18, 1988.

After marrying Charlie, Mona moved to a patrol cabin, from which point she joined Charlie on his backcountry patrol work. Her experience as a guide came in handy on patrol; she also proved herself adept at other backcountry tasks, such as handling horses and fighting fires. When Charlie retired in 1937, the Mathesons bought a Jasper riding stable from which they took groups out on outfitted trips. Three years later, they established the Circle M Guest Ranch just east of the park gates. They operated the ranch until 1952, when they moved to a small cabin across the road. They had one son, Glenn. Mona died on June 20, 1983.

(l–r) Charlie Matheson, Gwen Pickford, Charles Golden, Agnes Harragin and Mona Harragin. The Harragin sisters were the first licensed female guides in the national parks. The sisters later married local men and spent their lives in the Jasper–Hinton area.

to its south end. Saddle and pack horses were then used to transport visitors the remainder of the distance to Maligne Lake – the entire trip now taking only one day. (The trail from Medicine Lake south to the Evelyn Creek valley fell into disuse and is no longer in existence.) Ten years later, tourists could drive to Medicine Lake, put their car on a ferry to cross the lake then drive to Maligne Lake – all in only three hours.

Once the portion up the north side of Medicine Lake and on to Maligne Lake along the river was completed in 1918, the trail also started to see some use by groups travelling beyond the lake. In 1923 Jasper outfitter Jack Brewster initiated his three-week Glacier Trail pack-train trip from Jasper to Lake Louise and back.[19] The first section of the trip followed the new trail to Maligne Lake. Parties continued along Mary Schäffer's trail over Jonas Pass to the Brazeau River then turned west to cross Nigel Pass to the Columbia Icefield.[20] From there, the tours followed the Bow River to Lake Louise. Tent camps were set up along the way for the guests' convenience, and a three-day layover at the icefield allowed guests to explore the glacier – including a trip up the Alexandra and Castleguard rivers to the Castleguard Meadows.[21] The tours remained popular until the onset of the Great Depression in 1929.

Brewster's 1927 Glacier Trail trip was described in detail by participant Joan Robson, in an essay written in 1952.[22] Jack Brewster led the trip, assisted by wranglers Dorrel Shovar and Felix Plante and cook Carl Madsen. The paying customers were Mr. and Mrs. S.C. Edmonds of Philadelphia, Otto and George Schultz of Chicago, and Joan Robson of Jasper. Between them they had nine saddle horses and ten pack horses. The party left Jasper on July 3, spending the first night camped at Medicine Lake. The next day they moved on to Maligne Lake, where they spent a day before proceeding to camp on Maligne Pass the following night. July 7 found them at Waterfalls Campground on Poboktan Creek. The next day they crossed Poboktan Ridge (Jonas Shoulder) and camped on the Brazeau River. Following the river upstream almost to its headwaters took them off Old Klyne's Trail to Nigel Pass. They crossed the pass and continued to Camp Parker, where they camped on July 9. The following day they crossed Nigel Creek and climbed Parker Ridge to get a good view of the Saskatchewan Glacier before return-

Route III

Joan Robson, a long-time resident of Hinton, Alberta, participated in the 1927 Glacier Trail trip.

Jack Brewster, who initiated the Glacier Trail pack-train trips from Jasper to Lake Louise, is seen here on his July 1927 trip.

ing to Camp Parker. By July 23, they had reached Lake Louise.

Four years earlier, Caroline Hinman's Off the Beaten Track tour participants had seen Maligne Lake as part of a six-week journey. In the summer of 1923, Hinman led a pack train of 23 pack horses and 17 saddle horses along the route. Guide Curly Phillips, cook Jack Jensen and helpers Ed Neighbour, David and Frank Moberly, and Lewis Swift all contributed to the trip's success. Hinman's ten guests, including her sister and two men, arrived in Jasper on July 23. The horses and guides were ready and waiting. The party proceeded up the Maligne River, eventually reaching Maligne Lake. Following Hinman's custom of having a layover in particularly beautiful spots, the party was able to enjoy a few days on the shores of this northern gem. They then proceeded along Mary Schäffer's route over Maligne Pass to Poboktan Creek, where they turned west toward Fortress Lake and eventually Athabasca Pass, Tonquin Pass and back to Jasper.[23] There was no trail for the portion of the trip from Athabasca Pass to Tonquin Pass along the Continental Divide, and it required all of Curly Phillips's skill to find a route for the travellers.[24] There is still no trail there today.

In August 1924, a most unusual pair of tourists made their way to Maligne

Lake. Lawren Harris and A.Y. Jackson, members of the now-famous Group of Seven, arrived in Jasper to paint for the Canadian National Railway.[25] Not finding the scenery along the railway or around Jasper Park Lodge particularly interesting, they arranged to visit the backcountry. Park Superintendent Colonel Maynard Rogers had wardens transport the artists' supplies to Maligne Lake, while they themselves walked in.

Jackson and Harris began their quest for paintable scenery by borrowing a canoe and paddling to the end of the lake. Deciding that the mountains of the Colin Range to the east looked more appealing, they piled their supplies on a horse borrowed from the warden, climbed to the treeline and set up camp.[26] Jackson explained that "it was not easy to establish a camp there. We could find no level ground for the tent. The first night I rolled out of it, and next morning Harris found me some distance below, lying sound asleep against a tree."[27]

Despite the difficulties, they found the area to their liking: "the Colin Range was an amazing place, a kind of cubists' paradise full of geometric formations, all waiting for the abstract painter."[28] The location was so conducive to their work that they returned later in the summer, following visits to the Tonquin and Athabasca valleys. They returned to Jasper along the Shovel Pass route.[29]

COLEMAN'S CLINE RIVER, CATARACT AND JONAS PASSES SECTION

The southern end of Old Klyne's Trail runs from Poboktan Creek over Jonas Shoulder and Pass to the Brazeau River and on to its headwaters near the base of Cataract Pass. It continues over Cataract Pass and down Cataract Creek to the Cline River (near Pinto Lake) and finally down the Cline River to the Kootenay Plains. The first person to record using this part of the trail was L.Q. Coleman, only because of a detour.[30] As the Coleman brothers attempted to reach Athabasca Pass in 1892, a member of their party, Mr. Pruyn, fell gravely ill.[31] Lucius Coleman and Native guide Jimmy Jacob took the sick man from the Brazeau River back to Morley over Job Pass.[32] On their return, the pair headed northwest from the Kootenay Plains up the Cline River and over Cataract Pass to the headwaters of the Brazeau, two passes that Jacob had heard of but never previously used. They followed the Brazeau downstream until July 10, when they met up with the remainder of the group at a camp near Brazeau Lake. The reunited party then travelled northwest along Duncan McGillivray's old trail over Poboktan Pass and on to the Sunwapta.[33]

The Coleman brothers, accompanied by their friend Professor Lewis Stewart and young Morley rancher Frank Sibbald, headed back through the mountains in 1893. They set out along the foothills to the Red Deer River then crossed Divide Summit and Indianhead Pass on the now well-used route to the Kootenay Plains.[34] They intended to follow the Coleman–Jacob route over Cataract Pass to the headwaters of the Brazeau River then use a map Stoney Chief Jonas had drawn earlier in the trip to explore a new pass that would lead them to the Sunwapta River.[35]

At the Kootenay Plains, they crossed to the north side of the North Saskatchewan River. To reach the valley of the Cataract (Cline) River, they then " ... had to scramble down into the Coral Creek canyon, ford the rapid stream, and climb the opposite wall, coming out well above the

Artist A.Y. Jackson, who painted in the Rockies in the 1920s, returned to teach at the Banff School of Fine Arts. He is shown here (centre, front row) with the staff of the school, ca. 1940.

Above: Coleman's Pinto Lake, "an exquisite lake about a mile long and broad," as seen in the early morning.

Below: This startled moose makes its way quickly along the shallow shore of Pinto Lake.

river in a wide U-shaped valley, with Sentinel mountain behind us."[36] Following the Cline River to Cataract Creek was relatively easy. Then, rather than turning north up Cataract Creek toward the Brazeau, the Coleman party continued a short distance along the Cline River to find "a splendid valley to the south, where it [the river] begins in an exquisite lake about a mile long and broad, fed by an enormous spring forty feet wide. Pinto Lake, as we named it, is 5850 feet above the sea, and on three sides of it mountain walls rise to seven or eight thousand feet, making a wonderful amphitheatre."[37] The lake's name was inspired by the Colemans' most cantankerous pony, who subsequently went missing. Since the loads were light and the pinto was no one's favourite, they decided to leave him behind. Still, "though he was more trouble as a packhorse than all the others put together, [they] immortalised him by giving his name to an exquisite lake near the head of Cataract [Cline] River."[38]

From Pinto Lake, the Coleman party backtracked to Cataract Creek and continued over Cataract Pass to the headwaters of the Brazeau River. In order to find the new pass shown on Chief Jonas's map, they first climbed a steep snowy ridge at nine thousand feet (2743 m). It did not give any indication as to the location of the pass so they:

> ... climbed a higher mountain next day, a tilted block like all the peaks along the Brazeau, but so steeply tilted and with so rugged a surface of limestone that it was no 'sidewalk' to ascend. From the top we had one of the finest panoramas in the Rockies, for the Columbia Icefield with its surrounding peaks and glaciers was only ten or fifteen miles to the south-west, ... We could look down the whole length of the Brazeau valley and see the high, glacier-covered mountain north of Brazeau Lake, and we could look over into the head of the Sunwapta valley toward the north-west. From this high point we could see a valley crossing from near our camp toward a creek flowing into the Sunwapta, evidently the pass Jonas intended we should take, so that our plans were settled.[39]

They soon found a well-beaten blazed trail leading over the pass to the creek flowing northwest. Coleman named the creek and pass after Chief Jonas. Then came:

> a terrible bit of travel down Jonas Creek to the Sunwapta, when we alternately splashed through muskegs with sharp stones beneath the moss, and climbed up steep, rocky banks to escape them.... Things grew even worse lower down the valley, for there the woods were burnt and the fire had consumed the moss, leaving sharp rocks and fallen logs instead of a trail. ... every one was relieved when we came out of the rocky gorge into the gentler slopes of the Sunwapta valley.[40]

Though the Coleman party used the same route on their return trip in September, there is no report of anyone else using the difficult trail down Jonas Creek, and there is no trail there today. Klyne's alternative, a connecting trail from Jonas Creek over a ridge (Jonas Shoulder) to the Poboktan Creek trail, was rediscovered by guide Sid Unwin in 1914, when he was guiding American professor B.W. Mitchell on a pleasure trip through the area.[41] Unwin's pioneering of the Jonas Shoulder route and the Colemans' use of the Cline River–Cataract Creek and Pass route completed the rediscovery of Michael Klyne's trail between Poboktan Creek and the Kootenay Plains. Klyne himself had no doubt been following an old Native route, likely with Native guides; the Stoneys were still using these trails when the Colemans first used them.

In 1902 the Colemans returned to further explore the region between the Kootenay Plains and the Brazeau River. They chose to return along the Cataract Pass section of Old Klyne's Trail, which they had last used nine years earlier. They found the trail:

> ... in worse condition than in former years from the fall of trees. It seemed to have been very little travelled since our last journey, perhaps because Job Beaver, the man of energy

in his tribe, was no longer with the living. The events of the way, the usual incidents of rapid mountain travel with ponies, need not be recounted; but my brother and I looked with interest to the peak beyond Pinto Lake, marked Mount Coleman on Collie's excellent map.[42]

These pictographs, found on a large rock beside Cataract Creek, are not readily visible from the trail.

NIGEL AND SUNSET PASSES

Early travellers used two passes to cross from the North Saskatchewan River to the portion of Old Klyne's Trail south of the Brazeau River: Pinto (Sunset) Pass and Nigel Pass. When the Colemans first arrived at Pinto Lake in 1893, they spent a day exploring the area – including following a poorly marked trail to the top of the ridge overlooking the lake, from which they could see into the North Saskatchewan River valley. This is the first report of anyone crossing today's Sunset Pass, called Pinto Pass by early travellers.

It was on an 1898 hunting trip that mountaineer Hugh Stutfield and guide Bill Peyto made the first recorded crossing of Nigel Pass. Stutfield had been so impressed by the work of one of Peyto's men, Nigel Vavasour, in guiding him, J. Norman Collie and Herman Wooley on an earlier exploration trip to the Columbia Icefield, that he named the pass after him. English mountaineer-statesman Leopold Amery described the route from Nigel pass to Brazeau as "one of the loveliest rides in the whole of the Rockies."[43]

Mary Schäffer used both of these passes in her travels. In 1906 she, Mollie Adams, Billy Warren and Sid Unwin had travelled north along the Bow River to the Columbia Icefield.[44] They returned to Pinto Pass, crossed to Pinto Lake and followed Klyne's trail down the Cline River to the Kootenay Plains. Although this route to the Kootenay Plains was not widely used, Caroline Hinman essentially repeated Mary Schäffer's trip on her 1924 Off the Beaten Track tour. While at Pinto Lake, the group took a side trip to Cataract Pass before continuing down the Cline River.[45]

The Schäffer party crossed Nigel Pass again in 1907, this time headed for the Brazeau River after their explorations around Fortress Lake and Thompson Pass. After travelling along the Brazeau River to Brazeau Lake and exploring in that area, they returned almost to the top of Nigel Pass and set up camp near the base of Cataract Pass. They proceeded to follow Old Klyne's Trail north over Jonas Pass then returned to their camp and crossed Cataract Pass in heavy snow to arrive at Pinto Lake. The men crossed Pinto Pass to obtain food from a cache on the North

Saskatchewan River before continuing over well-worn Stoney trails along the Cline River to the Kootenay Plains.

The route was becoming popular. In 1908 Schäffer again used Nigel Pass at the beginning of the trip that led to the rediscovery of Maligne Lake.[46] Mrs. Crandell and Mrs. Chandler of Philadelphia followed suit when they retraced her route in 1914.[47] Their return trip involved a trip to Pinto Lake then following the Cline River downstream to the Kootenay Plains.

In 1909 a group on an epic journey from Lacombe, Alberta, to British Columbia's Fraser River reluctantly used Nigel Pass as an exit from the Brazeau drainage. Client Stanley Washburn, guide Fred Stephens, Fred's brother, Nick, as packer, a cook called Tom and a civil engineer named Sawyer (whom Washburn had managed to pick up at the last minute to make a map of the route) had brought 22 horses for the four-month expedition.[48] They headed north and west from Lacombe to the Brazeau River. At this point they proceeded to follow the river west then crossed a pass (most likely Poboktan Pass), which they hoped would take them to the Athabasca River. Thirty days into their journey they discovered that the route beyond the pass was blocked by a landslide, which forced them to return over the pass to the Brazeau and cross Nigel Pass to the North Saskatchewan.[49] By following the North Saskatchewan to Wilcox Pass, they were able to reach the Sunwapta River and eventually the Athabasca. By late August, they had succeeded in reaching the Fraser River, west of the Yellowhead Pass.

Wildlife artist Carl Rungius was the following summer's visitor of note in the area. As the Brazeau River basin was the favourite sheep-hunting area of outfitter Jimmy Simpson, it is no surprise that when Simpson convinced Rungius to visit the Rockies, he took the artist into the Brazeau River country.[50] In the fall of 1910, the pair headed north with packer Ernie Brearley. They travelled as far as Wilcox Pass then retreated to Nigel Pass to access the Brazeau River. Rungius's goal of finding material for his canvases was not thwarted; in addition to the sheep and goats he sketched, the party also encountered a grizzly near Jonas Pass. Rungius was so impressed with the area that he returned the following year with fellow artist Philip Goodwin.[51]

Carl Clemens Moritz Rungius (1869-1959)

Carl Rungius was born in Rixdorf (in what is now Berlin), Germany, in 1869. His early interest in both art and hunting eventually led to his lifelong commitment to painting wildlife in its natural habitat. While studying at the Berlin Art Academy, he also made time to sketch at the zoo. But he found that there were limited opportunities to fulfil his aspirations in Germany, as access to forests and undeveloped land was limited.

His horizons began to broaden in 1894, when he received an invitation from his uncle, Dr. Clemens Fulda, to hunt moose in Maine. Rungius jumped at the chance, and one thing led to another. At a sportsman show in New York, Rungius met Wyoming guide Ira Dodge. Rungius accepted his invitation to visit Wyoming, travelling west the following year. He spent five months stalking game and making detailed studies of his trophies. He used ropes suspended from a cross pole to rig an animal into a life-like position, after which he would paint it.

The following year, Rungius immigrated to the United States. Although he lived in New York with his uncle, he travelled to Wyoming nearly every year from 1896 to 1902 and again in 1915 and 1920. He also became acquainted with his cousin, Louise, and the two married in 1907.

In 1910 art-loving Canadian outfitter and hunting guide Jimmy Simpson invited Rungius to come to the Canadian Rockies to hunt and paint. Rungius was so taken with the area that in 1922 he bought a house and studio in Banff. He and Louise began to divide their year between Banff and New York City.

Rungius won several awards for his Canadian paintings. In 1922 his *Canadian Rockies* won best picture in the exhibition award at the Salmagundi Club. In 1925 his painting, *Lake McArthur*, won the prestigious Carnegie Prize, and the following year his

Mountaineer won the Popular Prize at the Corcoran Gallery in Washington, DC. The largest single collection of Rungius's work is held at the Glenbow Museum in Calgary, Alberta.

Rungius died in 1959 of a stroke while standing at his easel at home in New York City.

Wildlife artist Carl Rungius first came to the Canadian Rockies at the invitation of Jimmy Simpson. He became so enamoured with the scenery and wildlife that he eventually bought a seasonal home in Banff.

Rungius was not the only easterner captivated by the Brazeau River basin. Because the area was a favourite for hunting, both Stoneys and later outfitters took many visitors there, normally by crossing Nigel Pass from the North Saskatchewan River. Jimmy Simpson led a group of New Yorkers over Nigel Pass on September 1, 1915, proceeding over Jonas Pass and Shoulder and Poboktan Pass into the valley of Brazeau Lake.[52] They set up camp and spent the next two weeks hunting and enjoying camp life. In his diary, one of the group, Joseph McAleenan, recorded that:

> The campfire at night is fascinating. The flames leap, or drop and darken; the smoke changes, and we move lazily from one place to another as it shifts. There is a smell of burning wood. It is the hour for stories. No one seems afflicted with stage fright, and stories are told that never would be told at any other time and place. They belong to this campfire and hour.[53]

The following year, Simpson took another group of hunters to the Brazeau River country over Nigel Pass, this time assisted by Watty Failes as cook and Bob Alexander as wrangler. The clients, Robert Frothingham and George Martin, spent one month on the trail, mostly around their camp on Cataract Creek. Frothingham made his living writing and lecturing about the outdoors and relied on such trips to provide him with material for his stories. He was very complimentary toward his guide, claiming that Simpson "is, without doubt, the best hunter and most expert stalker of Bighorn Sheep in Western Canada."[54]

A little-known outfitter and explorer who played a prominent role in early travels in the Brazeau River country and along the Cline River was Clarence Sands. Sands began guiding and outfitting in 1919 and was somewhat unique in that he (like the Stoneys and the Coleman brothers before him) approached the mountains from the east. He trailed his pack string from his home base on a ranch near Rocky Mountain House, leading parties along the North Saskatchewan River to the Kootenay Plains and along Old Klyne's Trail to Pinto Lake. On some trips he ventured farther north along Coral and Job creeks into the Brazeau River country, no doubt using part of McGillivray's old trail.

Sands credited part of the success of his trips to what he considered to be a dying breed of horse: the cayuse. Cayuses, which were widely used by Natives and early outfitters, were Aboriginal-bred stock. Though they had a reputation for being unpredictable, they were often preferred for use in the mountains because their larger hoofs were a definite advantage in negotiating muskegs. Sands felt they were also superior to other horses in heavy deadfall and along steep rocky slopes – difficult terrain frequently encountered by early outfitters and their clients.[55]

The last people of note to cross Nigel Pass within the time constraints of this volume were honeymooners Cliff and Ruth Kopas, who crossed the pass and followed the Brazeau River to Brazeau Lake as part of their 1933 honeymoon horseback trip from southern Alberta to the Pacific Ocean. They returned to the Sunwapta along McGillivray's route and eventually reached Bella Coola at the Pacific Ocean after four months of travel.[56]

The Riviere family travelled with the Kopases on the last leg of their journey to Jasper, adding a light-hearted air to evening camps. In this playful camp scene, George Riviere is pretending to be a horse, with his wife, Maggie, and her sister, Annie, as riders. Ruth Kopas (in the white skirt) and the two men, Ray and Slim, enjoy the frolics.

MARY SCHÄFFER'S MALIGNE PASS SECTION

Mary Schäffer's 1908 rediscovery of Maligne Lake from the south began at Laggan (Lake Louise). Though it was her third significant trip north of the railway – and the second intended to scout out the lake – this time she and her party had a distinct advantage. "One of the greatest trophies we carried with us when leaving the next day for the North Fork of the Saskatchewan," Schäffer explained, "was a tiny grubby bit of paper on which Sampson [Beaver] had with much care traced the lake we had tried so hard to find, which was supposed to lie north of Brazeau Lake. He had been there but once, a child of fourteen, and now a man of thirty, he drew it from memory, – mountains, streams, and passes all included."[57]

They crossed Nigel Pass in the reverse direction from the previous year and followed a now well-used trail to Brazeau Lake. From there they followed in McGillivray and Coleman's footsteps over Poboktan Pass and along Poboktan Creek.[58] If they had continued following Poboktan Creek, they would have crossed the Endless Chain Ridge to arrive at the Sunwapta River, just as McGillivray and Coleman had done. But Beaver's map indicated that they should turn north at some point along the creek, following another creek that would lead them to a pass and the lake.

The party found that:

> The trail was a very well marked one till, on the second day's ride, it seemed to come to an abrupt end at the river's edge where there had been a large Indian camp at some time.... The Indians' map told us to leave the valley at the third creek coming in from the right. We had already passed a dozen of them and were now passing another, but no horse-feed was in sight. A short distance beyond, we reached an open stretch, found tepee-poles and stopped for the night.... With tents in order, all went off in as many different directions as possible.... Chief [Billy Warren] arrived [last] with the cheerful intelligence that 'we could still advance; a good trail led down the hill and was probably the real Pobokton trail.'[59]

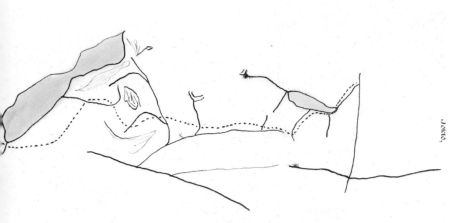

Having been to Maligne Lake as a child of 14, Stoney Sampson Beaver drew Mary Schäffer a rough map of the route from memory. Schäffer had met the Beaver family on an earlier visit to the Kootenay Plains.

The next morning dawned with six inches (15 centimetres) of snow covering everything in sight. After making their way down a tortuous trail to the creek bed, they

> ... again found old tepee-poles and a division of the way, one pointing to the Sun Wapta, the other leading into a notch in the hills with a northern trend. The stream from it really did seem as if it might be the one for which we were looking, and the opening in the hills the last possible one before reaching the end of the valley of the Sun Wapta.[60]

The decision was made to camp, and the

> ... household was getting into a rather divided state of mind, the opinion not having been unanimously in favour of this particular valley.... Consequently Chief and "K." [Sid Unwin] went off the next morning to see what was ahead.... At four

o'clock the men returned; had found a good trail, crossed a pass, could see miles ahead, but no lake of any description could be seen. The decision was to push ahead...[61]

The Schäffer party had found the right creek (Poligne Creek), which they followed to Maligne Pass. On reaching the eastern slope on July 6, Schäffer declared, "I think I never saw a fairer Valley. From our very feet it swept away onto an unbroken green carpet as far as the eye could see."[62] The next day they continued down the valley. After lunch

> ...up came the everlasting question: 'Where is that lake? Do you think we are on the right track?' "K.", who had grown more and more solemn for days, suddenly jumped up and shaking himself violently said; 'Well, it's two o'clock, but I'm going off to climb something that's high enough to see if that lake's within twenty miles of here, and I'm not coming back till I know!' ... The hours went by, ... and we all sat listening for the first crackle in the bushes. Not till 10:30 did it come, then he staggered out of the black forest into the flaring light ... with the joyful news, 'I've found the lake!' The quest was over, all doubts were at rest, so there was no turning back, we could go on.[63]

The next day they arrived at the lakeshore and located a good campsite with plenty of horse feed. After some investigation, Schäffer declared:

> Indians, of course, had been there, but, unless a prospector or timber-cruiser had come in by way of the Athabasca River, we had reason to feel we might be the first white people to have visited it. From the moment we left the trail on Pobokton Creek, there had not been one sign of a civilised hand; the Indian is a part of the whole, the white man, with his tin-cans and forest-fires, desecrates as he goes.... Yes, the long quest was over, the object found, and it seemed very beautiful to our partial eyes.[64]

As Mary Schäffer reached the top of Maligne Pass, she looked down and declared that she had never seen a fairer valley. It is not hard to see why.

Schäffer later grew very critical of those who felt she was trying to take credit for discovering Maligne Lake. She responded, "We never made any claims that 'we were the first people there.' One need only have followed our footsteps and seen the trapper's old campfires, the fallen wikkiups and many other marks to learn that the lake had been well visited long before the Indians told us of its beauty."[65] This statement was, of course, true. Michael Klyne's men had travelled back and forth from the Athabasca River to the North Saskatchewan between 1824 and 1835, using the route along the lake and over Maligne Pass. The area around the lake was regularly used by the Stoneys and by Métis from the Jasper area, and H.A.F. McLeod had visited the lake in 1875.

Four years after Schäffer's trip to Maligne Lake, Jack Brewster led a pack train from Lake Louise to Jasper. The party followed the Bow and Sunwapta rivers as far as Poboktan Creek, where they turned east along the McGillivray–Coleman route on Poboktan Creek.[66] No further details of this trip were recorded. It is clear that Brewster managed to find the creek leading north to Maligne Pass, but there is no indication of whether he experienced any difficulty finding Poligne Creek when approaching from the west.

In 1914 outfitter Jimmy Simpson led a pack train of 15 horses over the same route, escorting Mrs. Crandell of Philadelphia, who had planned to accompany Mary Schäffer in 1908 but had to withdraw because of illness. In spite of having discussed the route with Billy Warren and Sid Unwin and brought along the map from Mary Schäffer's book, the guides found they needed considerable route-finding skills to locate Poligne Creek as they travelled north from Poboktan Creek.

Parties heading south from Maligne Lake had a much easier time. In 1911 the Alpine Club of Canada's A.O. Wheeler had convened a large party at Maligne Lake as part of a combined Alpine Club of Canada and Smithsonian Institute of Washington, DC, expedition. Guide Curly Phillips, who became famous for his work in the Jasper area, noted in his diary that:

> Maligne Lake has no equal that I have ever seen. Water as clear as crystal stretched away for fifteen miles or more into the very heart of the range. The shore line is grand – points, bays, beaches, towering cliffs and great beaches of varied colours; and back and above it all dark green jackpines and spruce cover the mountains to treeline; while above it rise the snow covered peaks of the mountains.[67]

Wheeler had intended to make another great pioneering trip from Fitzhugh (Jasper) to Lake Louise, following in the footsteps of the Colemans, Brewsters and Schäffer, but the weather had other plans.

The first snow of the season fell on September 17, pushing Wheeler and the members of the Smithsonian Institute back to Fitzhugh. The ACC contingent was feeling more adventurous. Curly Phillips led mountain climber Reverend George Kinney, photographer Byron Harmon and Swiss guide Conrad Kain south over Maligne Pass. They left on September 18, crossing Maligne Pass to Poboktan Creek on the 19th. Phillips recorded:

> There is a good deal of soft ground on the Maligne river, but the worst trouble was the cripple brush out on the river flats, and the small knolls or mounds like ant hills. The pass is easy and very little above timberline, but there was about a foot of snow, so we had trouble keeping the trail.[68]

The snow continued the following day as they descended through fallen timber to Poboktan Creek. They then turned west to the Sunwapta, reaching Lake Louise in a total of 12 days. In early October, Phillips and Kain retraced their steps back to Fitzhugh. This time they spent 13 days on the trail, making them the first travellers to record completing the round trip from Fitzhugh to Laggan in less than a month.[69] Phillips noted that "the trip ... from Maligne Lake to Laggan ... is one of the most interesting in the mountains. The peaks all the way are high and very beautiful, a large number of glaciers being passed en route"[70] and predicted that "when a good trail is put through from steel to steel it will be very popular."[71]

Evidently the Brewster brothers agreed with this assessment; they initiated their Glacier Trail pack-train trip from Jasper to Lake Louise and back in 1923. Their route included Mary Schäffer's Maligne Lake to Poboktan Creek trail, as did Caroline Hinman's trips of 1923, 1925 and 1927.[72]

By 1969 federal authorities had developed plans to build a road from Maligne Lake to the Icefields Parkway (Sunwapta River) over Maligne Pass. The first step of the project was to build a highway bridge over the Maligne River at Maligne Lake. Fortunately, "negative public reaction regarding the loss of wilderness habitat, which would have threatened mammals like caribou and grizzly" prevented the project from proceeding any further.[73] Today's trail from Maligne Lake to Poboktan Creek is much as Mary Schäffer found it, albeit easier to follow.

The Trail Today

The first section of Old Klyne's Trail – the Harragin sisters' pack-train route from the Athabasca River to Medicine Lake, around the north shore of the lake and along the Maligne River to Maligne Lake – is now a high-speed road heavily used by visitors accessing the immensely popular Maligne Lake. Most of the old horse trail would have disappeared with road construction and the only possible foot-path along this route today is the shoulder of the road.

Upon reaching Maligne Lake by the road, however, hikers can retrace Mary Schäffer's route over the spectacular Maligne Pass to the trail junction on Poboktan Creek. Pausing at this junction, hikers can imagine what it would have been like for Billy Warren, Sid Unwin, Mary Schäffer and Mollie Adams to approach this meeting of three valleys, holding Sampson Beaver's hand-drawn map for direction. Their tense uncertainty as to which path would lead to the destination of their dreams is readily understandable: finding the right creek to follow north would take some skill without the Parks Canada sign and well-worn trail that are there today.

Once found, the area is unique, with Poboktan Creek flowing into a narrow valley from the southeast and flowing out to the west, and another stream coming in from the north. This junction also provides an easy exit for those wishing to do only this portion of the trail. For anyone who has arranged transportation, this is a very pleasant backcountry hike for all ages, there being no unusual challenges on this route. Several campsites are available along the route, as well.

Poboktan Creek also provides an easy entry for those wishing to hike from Poboktan Creek to Nigel Pass. This popular section of the trail is easy to follow, but its three high passes – Jonas Shoulder, Jonas Pass and Nigel Pass – make it somewhat strenuous for young hikers. The scenery is beautiful, campsites are provided, except on the Jonas Pass section where camping is not allowed, and all major streams are bridged.

I once stayed at the very popular Jonas Cutoff Campground in September, after the busy summer season was over. My expectation that the campground would be peaceful proved accurate; in fact, I was its only occupant. But there were other surprises in store for me. That afternoon and evening, I experienced an early heavy wet snowfall. The entire campground, which has virtually no grass cover, became unpleasantly muddy. Fortunately, my tent has a reasonably waterproof floor. By morning there were ten centimetres of snow on the ground, which made me worry about the trail over the very open heights of Jonas Shoulder. Fortunately, it did not prove to be a problem; because the season was early, the snow melted quickly.

For those wishing a more strenuous and challenging hike, either Poboktan Creek or Nigel Pass can be used to continue the hike over Cataract Pass to the Cline River. Portions of this route lack a defined trail, but route-finding is straightforward and relatively easy for those with some experience. Cataract Pass is steep and demanding, and most streams are not bridged, although the fords are not particularly difficult. The areas along the upper Brazeau River and Cataract Pass are exceptionally beautiful, as is the eastern side of the pass. The route down Cataract Creek, on the other hand, is heavily treed and relatively uninteresting.

At the junction with the Cline River, hikers have the option of exiting over Sunset Pass (originally called Pinto Pass) or continuing along the Cline River to the North Saskatchewan. Using Sunset Pass to join Old Klyne's Trail is another viable option; the Sunset Pass area is a worthwhile destination in itself, and anyone crossing the pass will want to visit Pinto Lake. But because of the high passes, the route-finding requirements and some difficult stream crossings, the Cataract Pass and Cline River portions of Old Klyne's Trail are most suitable for experienced backcountry travellers.

The hike down the Cline River is a pleasant river-valley hike, with at least two demanding creek fords: Cataract Creek, for those approaching from Sunset Pass, and McDonald Creek. As with many river-valley hikes, the open views allow hikers to enjoy fabulous mountain scenery. Unfortunately, this particular river-valley hike is spoiled by the constant drone of helicopters conducting circular sightseeing trips or ferrying tourists up the valley to a variety of destinations outside the national parks. Those wishing backcountry solitude will not find it here.

One of the most interesting parts of today's Nigel Pass trail is a stand of Engelmann spruce near the beginning of the trail. This is the site of old Camp Parker, thought to have been named after mountaineer Herschel C. Parker. The camp was used extensively by Native groups prior to the twentieth century and by early mountaineers and explorers after the coming of the railway. It is fascinating to look at the carvings on the trees, which record the visits of many of the early travellers, although many are from the post-1930s era. From Nigel Pass to Coral Creek along the Cline River route, there are no designated campsites, but there are several old outfitters' camps and random camping sites are plentiful along the Cline River section.

In the early days of pack-train travel, Camp Parker was a favourite stopping spot for parties heading northwest toward Wilcox Pass or north over Nigel Pass. Many of these travellers left their marks in the form of carved messages on trees, such as this one, which was still visible in 2008.

Trail Guide

Distances are adapted from existing trail guides: Patton and Robinson, Potter, and Beers, and from Gem Trek maps. Distances intermediate from those given in the sources are estimated from topographical maps and from hiking times. All distances are in kilometres.

From Maligne Lake over Jonas and Cataract Passes to the North Saskatchewan River

Maps   83 C/1 Whiterabbit Creek
83 C/2 Cline River
83 C/3 Columbia Icefield
83 C/6 Sunwapta Peak
83 C/11 Southesk Lake
83 C/12 Athabasca Falls
83 C/13 Medicine Lake
83 D/16 Jasper
Jasper and Maligne Lake (Gem Trek)
Columbia Icefield (Gem Trek)

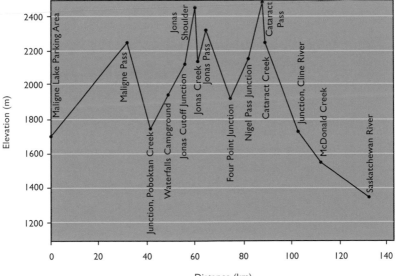

Trailhead

From Jasper, proceed north along Highway 16, turn right on the Maligne Lake road and follow it to the lake. Cross the outlet stream bridge and proceed to the last parking lot. The trailhead is at the south end of the parking lot. The trailhead at the south end of the trail is the Cline River trailhead described in the Job Pass hike in Route 11 above.

0.0   Trail starts out on a gravel road: the Bald Hills trail. Soon, turn left (south). After about 1 km the Moose Lake trail branches to the left (east). Continue ahead for Maligne Pass. The trail gradually climbs to the top of a ridge then drops down through the forest to Trapper Creek.

4.8   Trapper Creek Campground. Continue along the left (east) side of a long meadow.

8.7   Cross a side stream twice on bridges. Continue mostly through the meadow, sometimes entering the forest.

13.9   Footbridge across the Maligne River. Continue along the meadow then into the forest before emerging from the forest along the river.

18.9   Mary Schäffer Campground. Continue along the open area, then go into the trees.

24.2   Cross a bridge over a major stream coming in from the left (northeast). Continue through the forest then onto an open meadow with good views.

26.8   Old Horse campsite. Continue mainly along the meadow, with one section in the forest.

29.3   Mary Vaux Campground. Leaving the campground, the trail passes a big rockslide on the right side of the creek then starts climbing through a fairly open area toward the pass. This is a very beautiful area with great views of the surrounding mountains.

32.7   Maligne Pass. There is no marker here, but the top of the pass is near the north end of a charming lake. The trail continues past the lake to the right (southwest). The fine scenery continues as the trail steadily drops.

36.7   Avalanche Campground. From here the trail essentially follows a small creek, initially through a very open area but gradually into the trees as the trail descends toward Poboktan Creek.

41.7   Trail junction at Poboktan Creek. The trail to the right (west) leads along the creek to the Sunwapta River. Turn left (east) to travel upstream along Poboktan Creek. Continue on a good trail through the forest.

43.0   Poboktan Creek Campground. Just beyond the campground, a major stream comes in from the left and splits into two, with bridges across both branches. Continue through the forest on a good trail, cross a bridge over a side stream coming in from the left (northeast) and pass through a gate in a pole fence. Cross another creek on a bridge.

47.5   Waterfalls Campground. Continue along the valley-bottom trail.

49.1   Waterfalls Warden Cabin. Continue through a treed area with frequent good views.

49.7   Side stream with a bridge across it. The trail continues along the side of the Poboktan Creek valley, quite open and very beautiful.

55.2   Sign in a tree points to the McCready horse camp to the left. Continue ahead (southeast) and pass an old campground that has been closed.

56.8   Jonas Cutoff Campground. The trail ahead (east) goes to Poboktan Pass. Turn right (south) and follow the trail toward Jonas Shoulder. The trail immediately begins climbing through an open forest but soon reaches a very open area, where it continues to climb. Rock cairns help mark the trail.

60.1   Top of a high ridge. A sign reads: Jonas Shoulder, 2450 m. This is a very beautiful area. The trail drops diagonally down the side of the ridge to the valley bottom. It is very open all the way down.

Continue through a narrow valley then start climbing the gentle approach to Jonas Pass.

65.9   Jonas Pass, marked by a cairn with elk antlers on top. The pass is very open and flat with a dramatic mountain range on the right (southwest). The trail drops down through a fairly narrow valley with rocky ridges on either side. Trees gradually appear, but the trail remains very open.

71.6   Cross several streams in this area. One on the right has a pretty waterfall flowing over rocks. The trail continues parallel to Four Point Creek but high above it. The mountains on the southeast side of the Brazeau valley are visible. The forest becomes more mature as the trail approaches the Brazeau River, where it drops quite steeply.

75.7   Junction with the Brazeau River trail. Turn right (west) upstream along the Brazeau.

75.9   Four Point Campground. The trail follows along the river in an open scenic meadow. Climb over a forested ridge and cross Boulder Creek on a bridge.

79.0   Boulder Creek Campground. Just beyond the campground, the trail crosses the river on a bridge. Traverse a broad meadow then start the steep climb toward Nigel Pass. The trail climbs a steep barren rocky ridge. Near the top, the trail splits. Keep left and continue to climb along this rocky rugged area with great views of towering mountains. The trail drops down to the river.

82.2   Brazeau River. The trail to Nigel Pass crosses the river straight ahead (south). Turn left (southeast) along the bank of the river without crossing it, heading toward Cataract Pass. There are no signs directing hikers to the pass. The trail follows the edge of the river, sometimes avoiding marshy areas by detouring over rocky ridges marked by cairns. The trail is easy to follow. At the end of the river flats, it climbs to the left over a steep shale slope marked with cairns. You will soon see a large lake on the right (south), the source of the Brazeau River. Start a steep climb over a shale slope to the top of the pass. The trail is not always obvious, but the top of the pass is, and it is only necessary to keep climbing.

88.0 Top of Cataract Pass, marked with a cairn. A short distance ahead is a sign that reads: "Wilderness Area." Continue ahead; the trail keeps to the left (north) along a ridge to avoid a gully on the right. Once you can see the green valley of Cataract Creek down below, keep to the right, follow a depression, cross it and descend the right side of a dry creek bed.

89.6 Cataract Creek. Cross the creek on stepping stones. From here you have two choices. One is simply to follow along the northeast bank of the creek through fairly open forest and eventually (in an hour or more) come to a good trail in the woods heading downstream. The other option is to walk directly ahead (northeast), perpendicular to the creek across an open meadow-like area to intersect the horse trail from Cataract Creek to Cline Pass. It should take about 30 minutes to reach the trail. We recommend the latter option. Either way, you are in the narrow Cataract Creek valley and cannot go astray, especially if you watch your compass. Once on the horse trail, follow it southeast downstream along the creek, generally in the woods. Eventually the trail reaches the willow flats along the creek – a very open area with great views – then enters the open forest along the creek.

100.9 Campsite in the trees near the creek. The trail continues in the forest, past a rockslide and sheer rock wall on the left.

103.0 Trail splits. Keep left (southeast) through a forested area to reach the Cline River.

104.5 Cline River, flowing slightly north of east. From here, the trail follows the banks of the river. It is generally open with good views of the river and surrounding mountains.

113.9   McDonald Creek ford. The fast-flowing creek is thigh-deep, with a lot of boulders in the creek bed. This difficult crossing requires care. A second crossing of a side stream can be done on the rocks. The trail goes inland, avoiding a deep canyon, then reaches a boulder-filled floodplain.

119.0   Boulder Creek ford, calf-deep. There is a long climb up from the creek then the trail continues downhill, mainly in the trees.

125.0   Outfitter's camp. The trail ahead has been cleared as far as the camp. Continue in the forest.

127.4   Whitegoat Wilderness Area boundary. Continue through the forest.

128.4   Coral Creek ford, easy (calf-deep). After crossing the creek, there is a trail junction and campsite. The trail to the left goes to Job Pass. Keep right (east) for the North Saskatchewan River. Climb to the top of the bank then continue downhill on a wide, heavily used trail.

132.5   Trailhead parking lot and Highway 11, the David Thompson Highway.

From the Icefields Parkway over Nigel Pass to the Brazeau River

Maps   83 C/3 Columbia Icefield
Columbia Icefield (Gem Trek)

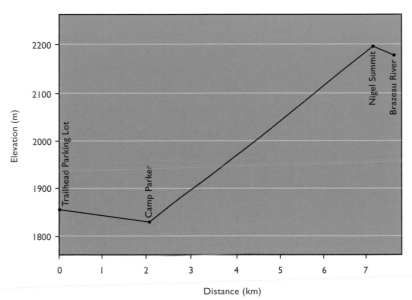

Trailhead

The trailhead parking lot is on the northeast side of the highway north of the Big Bend in the Icefields Parkway, 8.5 km south of the Banff–Jasper National Park boundary. Take the gravel side road that leads to the parking lot and trailhead. The east end of the trail is kilometre 82.2 of Old Klyne's Trail (see Route III above).

0.0   The parking area is quite scenic. The trail soon turns to the right (east) and crosses Nigel Creek on a footbridge. It then follows parallel to the creek, initially northwest. There are large open areas, with views of Parker Ridge dominant in the southwest.

2.1   Camp Parker. There are many blazes and tree markers along the trail in this old camping area. The trail continues along the creek with many open areas, avalanche slopes and good views of surrounding mountains.

5.1   Start of open meadows. The horse trail branches left (west) and later rejoins the hiking trail. The rocky ridge ahead marks the beginning of the climb to the pass. The trail keeps to the right (northeast) and winds around the edge of the ridge.

7.2   Nigel Summit. There is a steel Parks post here, but the sign has been removed. From the ridge, the trail drops down into a narrow rocky valley with a creek at the bottom.

7.6   Brazeau River, near its headwaters. This is a very scenic area.

This view shows the Brazeau River taken from near the top of Nigel Pass, looking north. The river drops rapidly from its rocky and barren heights to the valley below, where it flows northeast at a more leisurely pace.

From the Icefields Parkway over Sunset Pass to Cataract Creek

Maps   83 C/2 Cline River

Bow Lake and Saskatchewan Crossing (Gem Trek)

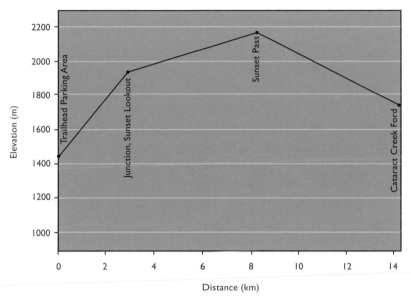

Trailhead

The trailhead is on the northeast side of the Icefields Parkway (#93), 16.5 km north of the junction with Highway 11 at The Crossing Resort. The parking lot is in an open area adjacent to the highway. Though it is not signed from the highway, it is clearly visible.

0.0   Trailhead signboard. The trail climbs steeply through the trees.

1.0   Viewpoint for Norman Creek gorge. The creek rushes down through a narrow rocky gully with a good view over the North Saskatchewan River valley to the south. The trail continues to climb steeply with switchbacks, offering good views to the south.

2.9   Trail junction. Sunset Lookout is on the left. A white painted sign points ahead to Norman Lake, Sunset Pass and Pinto Lake. Continue to climb; cross a minor ridge with a small pond on the left (north).

3.9   Climb another ridge with a view out over a long flat meadow. Come to a sign pointing to a campground.

4.4   Cross Norman Creek on a bridge. Norman Creek Campground is 100 m ahead. The trail continues along the meadow then through some open forest.

6.0   Cross a small ridge. A sign here says: "Sunset Pass left." The trail continues along the meadow with great views all around, especially of Mount Coleman to the northwest.

6.6   End of the meadow. The trail enters the forest and begins climbing toward the pass. Reach the top of a ridge.

8.2   Sunset Pass and national park boundary. A sign here reads: "area cleaned by volunteers, please keep clean." There is a good view of the Cline River valley. The trail turns to the left (northwest) then curves to the northeast and skirts around a rocky hummock.

9.7   Top of a ridge: rock cairn with views of Pinto Lake and the Cline River valley. The trail progresses slightly downhill and crosses an avalanche slope. The terrain is still very open.

11.2   Trail drops steeply through heavy forest, often with switchbacks. There are no views. Eventually you reach a low swampy area.

13.1   Trail turns to the left (northeast). There is an arrow on the ground made from small rocks pointing into a wet area to the right, which leads to the Pinto Lake Campground.

        If you want to go to Pinto Lake, follow the trail that is essentially parallel with the outflow from the lake. Proceed through the initial wet area and soon reach a well-used trail that continues to the lake in about 15 minutes.

To by-pass the lake and proceed toward Cataract Creek, continue to the northeast along the Cline River; come to an old outfitter's camp in 300 m.

13.8   Whitegoat Wilderness Area boundary sign. Continue along the river.

14.4   Cataract Creek ford, up to knee-deep. Downstream is a Whitegoat Wilderness sign. You have two choices at this point.

If you wish to go north along Cataract Creek, you can follow a faint trail on the east side of the creek and in about ten minutes join up with the main trail along Cataract Creek.

If you would rather continue along the Cline River, turning right at this trail junction is a good option. Another option is to follow the Cline River. Although there is no trail, it is fairly easy going, and you will join up with the trail coming down from Cataract Creek in about 45 minutes (see trail guide above, From Maligne Lake over Jonas and Cataract Passes to the North Saskatchewan River, kilometre 103).

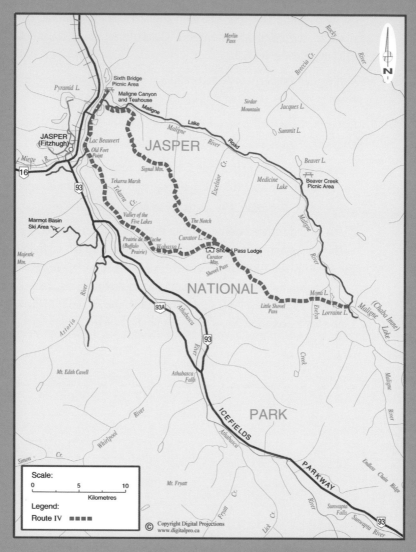

The Schäffer–Brewster routes from the
Athabasca River to Maligne Lake.

Route IV

Snow Shovels and High Passes: The Schäffer–Brewster Routes from the Athabasca River to Maligne Lake

Several years ago, my wife, Cheryl; daughters, Janice (co-author) and Susan; and I accompanied a family of four French friends on a three-day backpacking trip over the Skyline Trail. Like many inexperienced back-packers, our friends burdened their packs with too much paraphernalia. We redistributed gear early in the hike, leaving everyone with very heavy packs. The trail up The Notch was extremely slow and demanding, but everyone soldiered on without a word of complaint. Our guests had hiked extensively in France, Spain and Italy, but this was their first major outing in the Canadian Rockies. After taking a few minutes to catch his breath at the top of The Notch, the father declared the view out over the Athabasca River valley the most spectacular that he had ever witnessed. He then produced a video camera from his overloaded pack to film the scene. We were truly amazed that he had carried this heavy camera (this was before the days of the mini digital video cameras we all know) all that distance without mentioning it, but we were very happy that he could film the scenery that obviously brought him such delight.

CHRONOLOGY

1911   To facilitate a survey of Maligne Lake, Commissioner of Dominion Parks Howard Douglas agrees to have a trail cut from the proposed rail line in Jasper south along the Athabasca River to Buffalo Prairie then east along Wabasso Creek over today's Shovel Pass to the lake. Mary Schäffer conducts the survey, accompanied by her sister-in-law, Mrs. Caroline Sharpless; her nephew, Paul Sharpless; and guides Jack Otto and Sid Unwin.

In September James Shand-Harvey guides surveyor Arthur Wheeler, photographer Byron Harmon and Smithsonian members Harry Blagden and Charles Walcott up Curator Mountain and over Shovel Pass to Maligne Lake. Later that month, Curly Phillips follows, with Reverend George Kinney and Conrad Kain.

1913   Lawrence Burpee travels with pack train, guide and helper along an excellent trail through Buffalo Prairie and over what he calls Bighorn Pass (Shovel Pass) to Maligne Lake. He continues toward Medicine Lake over a somewhat difficult trail, marked by only a few blazes, takes a side trip to Jacques Lake and returns to Jasper over a difficult route along the Maligne River.

1914   From Jasper, a trail is cut up Signal Mountain to string a single telephone line over which fire ranger stations can communicate with each other.

1915   Surveyor M.P. Bridgland uses the Signal Mountain trail to begin his topographic survey of Jasper and the surrounding area.

1919   The trail up Signal Mountain is further cut out and improved.

1923   Fred Brewster sets up a circle tour from Jasper up the Maligne River to the lake, returning over Shovel Pass.

1924   Painters Lawren Harris and A.Y. Jackson make their way up the Maligne River on foot and spend some time painting in the vicinity of Maligne Lake. They return to Jasper over Shovel Pass led by a young guide, Don Ferris.

1925   The Jasper squadron of the Trail Riders of the Canadian Rockies make the circle trip up the Maligne River and hold a powwow on the shores of Maligne Lake. The following day, the party proceeds to Buffalo Prairie over Shovel Pass.

1933   Fred Brewster lays out the Skyline Trail route from Curator Mountain over the very steep Notch and along a series of high ridges to connect to the Signal Mountain trail. Brewster tests the route with horses, and by 1937 he feels that he can safely take tourists over the route.

Much of the Skyline Trail Fred Brewster laid out in the 1930s follows high ridges well above the treeline. During storms, hikers are at the mercy of Mother Nature.

HISTORY

CURATOR MOUNTAIN

Mary Schäffer's historic 1908 journey to Maligne Lake aroused enough interest in Ottawa that the commissioner of Dominion Parks, Howard Douglas, agreed to have a trail cut from the proposed rail line in Jasper south along the Athabasca River to Buffalo Prairie and east along Wabasso Creek over a high unnamed pass (Shovel Pass) to Maligne Lake.[1] The main purpose of cutting the trail was to allow the lake to be surveyed; why the route up Curator Mountain and over Shovel Pass was chosen remains a mystery. Although the Curator Mountain route must have been known and was most likely an old Native route, there is no previous report of anyone using it. The distance is roughly equivalent to the route up the Maligne River and the terrain is no easier. By 1914 a new trail had been cut as far as Medicine Lake, and by 1918 it stretched up the Maligne River to Maligne Lake. In the ensuing years, this trail was heavily used as the main route to the lake.

Government contractors cut the Curator Mountain trail from the Athabasca River to today's Skyline Trail to enable the Schäffer party to conduct its 1911 survey of Maligne Lake. From this vantage point on the Skyline Trail, the heavily used Curator Mountain Campground can be seen as an open spot in the trees on the left. Just below the campground, out of sight at the head of the meadow, is the Shovel Pass Lodge.

Mary Schäffer (1861-1939)

Mary Schäffer was born in West Chester, Pennsylvania, on October 4, 1861, to Alfred and Elizabeth Sharpless. She had a pampered childhood, growing up in a household full of maids and servants. Her primary and secondary school education, obtained at local public and private schools, was enriched by lessons with renowned flower painter George Lambden and time spent with her father, an amateur geologist, exploring the great outdoors.

As a girl she was fascinated by stories of Native Americans, and at age 14 she had the opportunity to travel west on the railroad. Though the trip was somewhat disillusioning, the reality of dispossessed Natives living in poverty did not dampen her enthusiasm for the indigenous peoples of the West. Throughout her youth, Schäffer's travels brought her in contact with a variety of Aboriginal peoples, and she carried her enthusiasm for them throughout her life.

On July 24, 1889, she married the twice-widowed Dr. Charles Schäffer and moved to Philadelphia. Early in their married life, Schäffer accompanied her husband to a scientific meeting in Toronto, then on to the Canadian Rockies. They returned to the Rockies two years later, establishing themselves at Glacier House on Rogers Pass. Charles's financial means and his passion for the flora of the Canadian Rockies combined to enable the couple to spend every summer in Mary's beloved Rockies, collecting botanical specimens that Mary dried, pressed, painted and photographed for Charles to identify.

Early in 1903, this idyllic life of stylish Philadelphia living in the winter and mountain touring in the summer came to a crashing halt. Within a few short months Schäffer lost her husband and both parents. In an attempt to overcome her grief and loneliness, the 42-year-old widow decided to try to complete the botanical guide she and Charles had dreamed of creating. She asked Stewardson Brown, curator of the herbarium at the Philadelphia Academy of Natural Sciences, who was familiar with and respected her husband's work, to collaborate with her

Mary Schäffer was the first non-Native woman to travel extensively in the Rocky Mountains. It was her party that rediscovered Maligne Lake from the south in 1908. The federal government asked her to survey the lake in 1911, and she was instrumental in having the area retained within Jasper National Park.

to this end. This brought her back to the Rockies and eventually led to the publication of *Alpine Flora of the Canadian Rocky Mountains*, written by Stewardson Brown with illustrations by Mary T.S. Schäffer.

Collecting the specimens required to complete the guide had forced Schäffer to overcome her fears of horses and camping. And when the book had gone to press, she went on to initiate two summer-long expeditions north of Laggan, the expeditions of 1907 and 1908. The latter year brought both fame and misfortune. Only months after she and her travelling companion Mollie Adams had accomplished their goal of rediscovering Maligne Lake, Adams contracted pneumonia and died. Schäffer's only subsequent trip of consequence was in 1911, when she complied with the Canadian government's request that she survey Maligne Lake.

Since her early years of widowhood, Schäffer had been sharing her adventures through writing and lantern slide shows. In 1911 she augmented this effort by publishing the extremely popular *Old Indian Trails of the Canadian Rockies*. The following year she had her own home built in Banff, where she took up permanent residence. On June 24, 1915, she married her mountain guide, Billy Warren.

In her later years, Mary became very involved in the Banff community. She was particularly fond of the town's youth and noted mountain people like old friends George, William and Mary Vaux, and Lillian Gest. She and her husband also found time to travel, especially winter trips to warmer climes. Mary died at home of pneumonia on January 23, 1939. She is fondly remembered as the first non-Native woman to explore many parts of the Canadian Rockies.

SURVEYS AND SHOVELS

The authorities' initial route selection saw Mary Schäffer; her sister-in-law, Mrs. Caroline Sharpless; and her nephew, Paul Sharpless, head up Curator Mountain in the summer of 1911. Their guides, Jack Otto and Sid Unwin, met the easterners at the end of steel in Hinton on June 7. The railroad was not the only development in the area; Jasper Collieries was nearby and the first two ladies to visit the establishment were invited for dinner. Schäffer says:

> we heard the musical sound of a triangle, and were asked if we minded eating at the same table with the miners, for they had no other place to offer us. Our appetites had reached such a condition, we minded nothing, but when we reached the dining room we found there was nothing to mind. I think they must have specially scrubbed those miners for the occasion; … and as for the dining room, it would have shamed some of those eastern architects who plan "bungalows" for ladies' magazines into retiring from business.[2]

As the ladies dined, the pack train had passed and camp been set up near the site of Jasper House. The party visited the ruins the next morning, only to find that "once there, there was little enough to see. All that marked the historic stop were the remains of some chimneys, a few logs tossed upon the ground, and a short distance from these, the ruins of an old grave-yard."[3] They resumed travel early the next morning, passing teams pulling loaded wagons heading west. After a brief stop at the homestead of Lewis Swift, a white man who had made a home in the Athabasca valley 18 years earlier, they proceeded to a campsite on the banks of the Athabasca. From there, they would proceed over the mountain passes to Maligne Lake.

The purpose of Mary Schäffer's 1911 trip to Maligne Lake was to survey the lake. Jonas was the unlucky horse relegated to carry the unwieldy planks (16 feet long, 18 inches wide, and over an inch thick) required to construct a boat. The fact that it was no easy task was highlighted when he tripped during a stream crossing, embedding the boards in the far bank and pinning his head underwater.

Their journey over the newly constructed trail was complicated by the necessity of carrying the 16-foot (5-metre) cedar planks from which their boat would be built once they reached Maligne Lake. A horse named Jonas was relegated the task. "His burden was lashed to his unprotesting sides," Schäffer explained, "a rope looped across the front end of the boards. Jack [Otto] assumed the position of steering gear, and Jonas acting as propeller, the pair took the lead of the small procession."[4]

Schäffer was thrilled to be on the trail again – and keen to share its wonders with her young nephew. However, not everything turned out to be as it appeared. "A mile from the summit, where the last, hard ascent began," Schäffer wrote, "Jack rather excitedly called our attention to two tiny specks on the skyline and, though he remained sweetly non-committal and suggested they might be a horse or two, we knew he meant 'sheep,' and sheep they promptly became."[5]

The weary travellers carried on, fuelled by the anticipation of what lay ahead. At last, Schäffer continued, "we came close enough to analyse our two immovable sheep – only to find them a pair of abandoned shovels which had been hewn from a tree and, in case we needed the same, left standing conspicuously in the snow.... [L]aughingly we named the pass 'Shovel Pass' and went on our way down the heather and snow decked slopes."[6] The shovels remained in place for many years, acting as sentinels to mark the top of the pass. Today they are in the Jasper museum.

The party eventually reached the lake on June 19; on July 25 the survey was complete, and Otto escorted the adventurers back to the railway.

Meanwhile, surveyor Arthur Wheeler and members of the Smithsonian Group were busy exploring the Mount Robson region. In late August, James Shand-Harvey guided Harry Blagden, Charles Walcott Jr. and Byron Harmon to Maligne Lake along the Curator Mountain route. A few weeks later, Curly Phillips followed with Arthur Wheeler, Reverend George Kinney and Conrad Kain.[7] Wheeler continued his survey south from Jasper to the lake but was very upset that a mere amateur had named Shovel Pass. He complained that "it is not a good name, and 'Bighorn Pass' would be a better one, for we saw flocks, aggregating thirty-five mountain sheep, in and around it, in three days."[8] Wheeler's name was used for a

Shovels, carved from a convenient tree, were
used to clear snow from the top of the pass.
From a distance, Mary Schäffer and companions mistook them for sheep.

few years, but Shovel Pass is the one that endured. Likewise, although Wheeler also suggested alternative names for features Schäffer had named around the lake, her nomenclature was officially recognized – it was a rare occasion when Wheeler did not get his way in naming alpine features.

Above: The route up Curator Mountain, taken from Curator Mountain Campground. The trail is still used today to service Shovel Pass Lodge, located to the left of the meadow shown.

Below: The faint trail leading up to Shovel Pass can be seen in the background to the left of centre.

Opposite: (l–r) Arthur Wheeler, Curly Phillips, Harry Blagden, J.H. Riley, Charles Walcott Jr., Reverend George Kinney (seated), James Shand-Harvey and Casey Jones were members of the 1911 ACC–Smithsonian party that explored in the Mount Robson and Maligne Lake areas.

CIRCLE TOURS

In 1913 Canadian historian, librarian and writer Lawrence Burpee travelled with pack train, guide and helper along what he described as an excellent trail through Buffalo Prairie and over what he called Bighorn Pass (Shovel Pass) to Maligne Lake. He continued toward Medicine Lake over a somewhat difficult trail, marked by only a few blazes "pointing the way through a perfect wilderness of fallen timber. How the ponies, with all their marvellous intelligence and matchless endurance dragged themselves and us through the miles of hopelessly tangled logs that covered ridge and valley nearly every foot of the way to Medicine Lake, none of us could ever understand."[9] Once at the lake, he took a side trip to Jacques Lake then returned to Jasper over a difficult route along the Maligne River.[10]

In 1924 painters Lawren Harris and A.Y. Jackson took advantage of the 1918 trail up the Maligne River to hike to Maligne Lake.[11] After spending some time painting in the vicinity, they returned to Jasper over Shovel Pass, led by a young guide, Don Ferris. Poor weather complicated the trip; a snowstorm forced them to spend a night camped near the top of the pass. Twenty-five years later, Jackson was flying over the Barren Lands of the Northwest Territories when the pilot of the plane, Don Ferris, asked him if he remembered going over Shovel Pass with an artist named Harris. Jackson did remember and Ferris revealed that he had been their guide.[12]

Lawren Stewart Harris (1885–1970)

Lawren Harris was born on October 23, 1885, in Brantford, Ontario. His family was conservative, religious and wealthy. As a founding member of the Massey-Harris (later Massey-Ferguson) farm implement company, his father, Thomas Morgan Harris, amassed a fortune. Consequently, Harris never had to work for a living and was able to devote his life to art. Up to 1904, he gained his early education at Toronto's St. Andrews College, after which he spent three years in Berlin, where he pursued interests in philosophy and Eastern thought. Back in Canada, his Berlin studies evolved into a fascination with theosophy (a philosophy professing to achieve knowledge of God by spiritual ecstasy, direct intuition or special individual relations) and membership in the Toronto Lodge of the International Theosophical Society.

On January 20, 1910, Harris married Beatrice (Trixie) Phillips. Over the next ten years, they had three children. In the meantime, however, Harris had met and fallen in love with Bess Houser, the wife of a high-school friend. Though they did not proceed with a liaison at the time, some 24 years after marrying Trixie, Harris left her to marry Bess.

Soon after his first marriage, Harris also met and befriended J.E.H. MacDonald. In 1911 the two teamed up with others to form the Group of Seven, which later expanded to ten artists devoted to a unique depiction of the Canadian landscape. In 1918 Harris financed box-car trips to the Algoma region of northern Ontario and later to the North Shore of Lake Superior. He was so taken with the area that he returned annually for the next seven years. He kept pushing the limits of his paintings, never being satisfied with one style or subject matter for very long. He led trips to the Rocky Mountains between 1924 and 1927, to the Gaspé between 1924 and 1930 and to the high Arctic in 1930.

Shortly after their 1934 marriage, Harris and Bess moved to New Hampshire. Four years later, they relocated to New Mexico, and then to Vancouver in 1940. Harris continued with his abstract style of painting, becoming a leading figure in the Vancouver arts community. In 1969 he was made a Companion of the Order of Canada. He died in Vancouver on January 29, 1970, a well-known and respected Canadian artist.

Lawren Harris, one of the best known of the artists of the Group of Seven, was a war artist between 1914 and 1918. He is seen here in army uniform with his paint box. His trips to the Rockies began less than a decade later.

In 1925 the Jasper squadron of the Trail Riders of the Canadian Rockies travelled up the Maligne River to the lake, where Major Fred Brewster called a powwow to order. The following day, they proceeded to Buffalo Prairie over Shovel Pass.[13] By the late 1920s, Fred Brewster had decided to take advantage of the lake's growing popularity by setting up a circle tour along this same route.[14]

THE SKYLINE TRAIL

The trail from Maligne Lake over Shovel Pass to Curator Mountain is part of today's popular Skyline Trail. Its north end from Jasper up Signal Mountain was begun in 1914, when a single telephone line was strung to the top to allow fire ranger stations to communicate with one another. Surveyor M.P. Bridgland used this trail to begin his topographic survey of Jasper Park and the surrounding area in 1915.[15]

Jasper outfitter Fred Brewster was the first to realize that the Signal Mountain trail might be connected with Schäffer's Curator Mountain survey trail. By 1933 he had laid out the Skyline Trail's present route from Curator Mountain over the very steep Notch and along a series of high ridges to connect up with the Signal Mountain trail. He tested the route with horses, and by 1937 he felt that he could safely take tourists over it. By 1941 he had taken 153 riders over the trail by horseback – a foretaste of the trail's current popularity.[16]

Opposite: Hikers make their way toward the snow-covered Notch, the steepest and most difficult part of the Skyline Trail.

Below: Beyond The Notch, the trail follows a series of high ridges then drops down into a valley. The trail can be seen on the left of the image, dropping rapidly to the valley floor through a series of switchbacks.

The Trail Today

When Mary Schäffer travelled in the Jasper area in 1911, she, her sister-in-law and nephew took the train to the end of steel in Hinton then travelled the remainder of the way by horseback. They crossed to the west side of the Athabasca to pay a brief visit to the Swifts then crossed the river again somewhere south of the mouth of the Maligne River, avoiding another potentially difficult crossing. Schäffer's trail is very similar to the one described here, which begins where the Maligne River meets the Athabasca.

The trail along the Athabasca from the Maligne River to Old Fort Point is heavily used today, primarily by cyclists. Because there is virtually no elevation change and there are many points where hikers can join and exit, this makes a pleasant hike for families, especially those staying nearby. Tucked between the developed areas around the lakes on the east and busy Highway 16 on the west, the route is not, however, as quiet as it would have been back in 1911.

The continuation of the trail from Old Fort Point past the Tekarra Meadows, the Valley of the Five Lakes and Prairie de la Vache (Buffalo Prairie) to Wabasso Lake is likely the route used by all early travellers trekking north along the Athabasca. It, too, is used mainly by cyclists but is not a particularly easy route. Its many steep hills and rough and rocky sections appeal to some but not all. I found it a difficult ride. There are easy access trails from the Icefields Parkway to the Valley of the Five Lakes and Wabasso Lake; these areas are heavily used by hikers of all ages.

Today, the trail up Curator Mountain is mainly used by horse parties ferrying customers to Shovel Pass Lodge (located near the top of the mountain, just below the intersection with the Skyline Trail). The trail could be used as an approach or exit point for part of the Skyline Trail, but the demanding hike up the mountain would not appeal to most. There are no campgrounds on this route between the Maligne River and Shovel Pass Lodge. Just above the lodge is Curator Campground, but as it is part of the busy Skyline Trail route, it is heavily booked during the summer months. Continuing along Schäffer's route over Shovel and Little Shovel passes to Maligne Lake is a very pleasant hike, which will appeal to a large number of people. Most of the hundreds of backpackers who hike the Skyline Trail each year will, however, choose to start at Maligne Lake and hike to Signal Mountain and on to Jasper.

Starting at Maligne Lake, the hike to Curator Mountain is more of a traditional mountain hike. Parts of it are above treeline, but there is vegetation throughout. Beyond Curator Mountain, the scenery becomes spectacular with views out over the Athabasca River valley and surrounding mountains. The trail is also above treeline and often devoid of vegetation, and the high ridges can be windy and demanding. My last trip was during inclement weather and was not pleasant in the exposed areas. But in spite of the area's starkness, the amazing views of the valleys and surrounding mountains reward the persistent hiker.

High passes along the entire route from Maligne Lake to the Maligne Lake Road make it a demanding trip, but there are no route-finding difficulties nor are there difficult streams to cross. The main limitations are the exposed areas during storms and the very busy summer season, when the campsites get booked up well in advance. I did the route as a day hike, which is a viable option for very strong hikers but not recommended for most.

From the top of The Notch, the Athabasca River valley west of Jasper can be seen clearly, with the Marmot Basin ski runs in the centre of the photo.

Trail Guide

Distances are adapted from existing trail guides: Patton and Robinson, Potter, and Beers, and from Gem-Trek maps. Distances intermediate from those given in the sources are estimated from topographical maps and from hiking times. All distances are in kilometres.

From the Athabasca River to Wabasso and Maligne Lakes

Maps   83 C/12 Athabasca Falls
         83 C/13 Medicine Lake
         83 D/16 Jasper
         Jasper and Maligne Lake (Gem Trek)

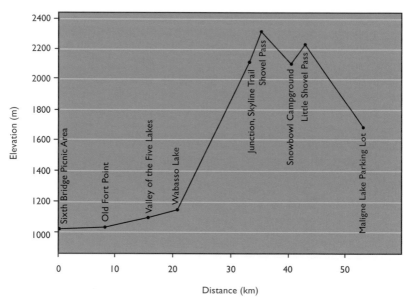

Trailhead

Follow Highway 16 north from Jasper, cross the Athabasca River on the Maligne Lake Road and follow it 2.6 km to the Sixth Bridge access road.

Turn left and follow the access road 1.6 km to the Sixth Bridge Picnic Area. This is the start of the hike and is close to where Mary Schäffer and her party would have crossed the Athabasca River. To begin at Maligne Lake and hike the trail in the reverse direction, continue on the Maligne Lake Road to the lake and cross the highway bridge across the Maligne River to the parking area. The trailhead is at the north end of the parking area.

0.0   Sixth Bridge Picnic Area. The trail (#7) follows the left (east) bank of the Athabasca River all the way to Old Fort Point. There are trail maps at various points along the way.

3.4   The trail crosses the Maligne Lake Road just after the road crosses the river and continues to follow the river.

7.0   Opposite Jasper Park Lodge. The trail passes Lac Beauvert and crosses a bridge over an outlet stream. There are many trails in this area. Keep right, close to the river on an old road, until you come to a bridge across the river and a roadway.

8.2   Old Fort Point. From here, take trail #1, which initially climbs on an old road. Come to a junction with trail #1A. Keep to the right on trail #1. The trail climbs to the top of a very steep ravine then drops.

9.7   Junction with trails #1A and #9. Keep straight ahead on #9, up several rough and rocky sections.

11.9   Junction with trail #9C, just before the Tekarra Marsh. The trail climbs two steep hills.

13.6   Junction with trail #9A, which goes left along the northeast side of the lakes. Keep to the right. The trail crosses a steep rough rocky ravine, passes a small lake on the right then leads through an aspen forest to a viewpoint overlooking Prairie de la Vache (Buffalo Prairie).

16.3   Junction with trail #9A. Turning right onto this trail leads to the Icefields Parkway in 1 km, providing an easy exit or access to the Valley of the Five Lakes. Continue straight ahead on trail #9, which follows a high ridge above the meadow then climbs a steep hill, passes a small lake on the left and continues through another meadow.

21.9   Junction of Wabasso Lake and the Curator Mountain trail. By turning right (southwest), this trail reaches the Icefields Parkway in 3.2 km and provides another exit–entrance point. Turn left on a well-used horse trail through a mixed aspen forest. You will come to a wide gravel section with blaze marks on the trees, cairns and yellow markers to guide you through. The trail veers to the left (east) then heads back into the trees to the right, eventually climbing to a good trail in the woods.

24.4   First switchback. The trail continues to climb steeply.

29.5   Old outfitter's camp, just after a fence and gate. Continue to climb through a narrow valley with steep mountain slopes on both sides and occasional views of Curator Mountain. The trail gradually levels out and you reach a small meadow.

31.9   Shovel Pass Lodge. Continue uphill.

32.3   Curator Campground, immediately above the lodge. A steep climb above the campground takes you above treeline.

33.8   Junction with the Skyline Trail. Turn right (southeast) and start climbing.

35.6   Top of Shovel Pass. 100 m farther is the junction with the Watchtower Trail, which branches to the left (north). From the top of the pass you can see the Marmot Basin ski area and fabulous views of the surrounding mountains. The trail drops gently through an open area. It has been ditched to overcome some very boggy areas.

41.3   Snowbowl Campground. Continue through open country, cross a major stream on rocks and follow the creek toward the pass, climbing steadily.

42.8   Little Shovel Pass. Very open and meadow-like with great views of the surrounding mountains. The trail then drops through another open area.

44.9   Little Shovel Campground. The trail drops through open forest. This is still a very scenic area.

48.1   Evelyn Creek Campground and bridge. Just after the bridge, the Bald Hills trail branches to the right. Continue ahead. After you reach a small lake on the right, a much larger lake is visible through the trees on the left (north).

50.8   Mona Lake trail branches to the left (north). Continue ahead.

51.1   Lorraine Lake trail branches to the right (south). Continue ahead.

53.1   Maligne Lake parking lot.

From Curator Mountain to Signal Mountain and the Maligne Lake Road

Maps   83 C/13 Medicine Lake
        83 D/16 Jasper
        Jasper and Maligne Lake (Gem Trek)

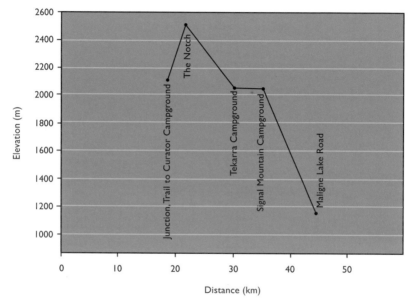

Trailhead

The beginning of the trail is at kilometre 33.8 of the Athabasca River to Curator Mountain and Maligne Lake trail above and is 19.3 km from Maligne Lake. The north end is at a parking lot on the Maligne Lake Road, 0.8 km south of the Maligne Canyon Teahouse and parking area.

19.3   Junction with the trail to the Curator Mountain Campground (the distance given [19.3 km] is the distance from Maligne Lake [see trail guide above]). Proceed northwest from the junction, to the left if coming from the campground, straight ahead if coming from Maligne Lake.

20.2   Curator Lake. Steady and steep uphill climb with switchbacks toward The Notch. There is often a snowbank near the top that can be crossed safely with due care.

22.0   Top of The Notch. This high barren ridge is a great viewpoint, especially for the Athabasca valley. The trail contours to the right (northwest) and reaches the top of a ridge with the beautiful valley of Excelsior Creek on the right. The trail continues along the ridge, passing two lakes, also on the right.

26.6   The trail starts to drop rapidly to a valley bottom.

28.1   Reach the valley bottom, which is still very barren and open.

29.5   Clump of trees next to a lake.

30.4   Tekarra Campground in a larger clump of trees. The trail climbs gently along a ridge above treeline. This is a great viewpoint for the Athabasca valley east of Jasper. The trail follows the ridge then starts dropping steadily into the forest and becomes an old road.

35.5   Signal Mountain Campground and junction to Signal Mountain Lookout site. The trail continues down the Signal Mountain fire road.

44.0   Maligne Lake Road and parking lot.

NOTES

INTRODUCTION

1 Mary T.S. Schäffer. Quoted in E.J. Hart, ed., *A Hunter of Peace: Mary T. S. Schäffer's Old Indian Trails of the Canadian Rockies* (Banff: the Whyte Foundation, 1980), i.

ROUTE I

1 For more details about this trip, see *Life of the Trail 1: Historic Hikes in Eastern Banff National Park* (Calgary: Rocky Mountain Books, 2008), 22–29.

2 Arthur S. Morton, "The Last of Fort George and Duncan M'Gillivray," *The Journal of Duncan M'Gillivray of the North West Company at Fort George on the Saskatchewan, 1794–5, With Introduction Notes and Appendix by Arthur S. Morton* (Macmillan of Canada, 1929), 8.

3 Le Grand Brazeau mountain range, which gave name to the river and lake, was named after Joseph Brazeau, a Hudson's Bay Company employee. Brazeau was an American Creole from Missouri, who spoke five indigenous languages, as well as English, Spanish and French. He entered the fur trade in 1830 and served as a clerk from 1852 to 1864 in Edmonton and at Rocky Mountain House and Jasper House.

4 Morton, 8–9.

5 Joyce and Peter McCart, *On the Road with David Thompson* (Calgary: Fifth House, 2000), 50.

6 A.P. Coleman, *The Canadian Rockies New & Old Trails* (Calgary: Aquila Books, 1999), 122.

7 Ibid.

8 Ibid.

9 Ibid, 134.

10 Ibid, 134–35.

11 Ibid, 137.

12 For details of the Job Pass trail, see Route II, on page 49.

13 For details of the Cataract Pass trail, see Route III, on page 99.

14 Coleman, 144.

15 Ibid, 145.

16 Ibid, 163. For details of the Job Pass trail see Route II, on page 49.

17 For more information see Route III, on page 132.

18 Janice Sanford Beck, *No Ordinary Woman: The Story of Mary Schäffer Warren* (Calgary: Rocky Mountain Books, 2001), 63.

19 For more information on this portion of the trip, see Route III, on page 132.

20 E.J. Hart, *Jimmy Simpson: Legend of the Rockies* (Canmore: Altitude, 1991), 118.

21 For a brief biographical sketch of Jimmy Simpson, see *Life of the Trail 3: The Historic Route from Old Bow Fort to Jasper* (Calgary: Rocky Mountain Books, 2009), 116.

22 Hart, 73.

23 Quoted in Hart, 73.

24 Hart, 74.

25 For more information about the Jonas Pass and Jonas Shoulder trail, see Route III, on pages 121, 130, 138, 144.

26 Lillian Gest fonds, Whyte Museum of the Canadian Rockies, M67/41, 32–38.

27 For more information about the Job Pass trail, see Route II, on page 49.

28 For more information about the portion of their trip along Old Klyne's Trail, see Route III, on page 121.

29 Quoted in Cyndi Smith, *Off the Beaten Track: Women Adventurers and Mountaineers in Western Canada* (Lake Louise: Coyote Books, 1989), 124.

30 For more detail about this portion of the trip, see *Life of the Trail 3*, 131.

31 Graveyard camp was so named by Mary Schäffer and party because of the large number of animal bones strewn about, attesting to the number of hunters who had camped there over the years.

32 For more information on Matheson and Harragin, see Route II, on page 71 and Route III, on pages 116-17.

33 Cliff Kopas, *Packhorses to the Pacific: A Wilderness Honeymoon* (Victoria: TouchWood Editions, 2004), 55–66.

34 For more information on the McGillivray–Southesk route, see Route II, on page 49.

35 For more information on the Job Pass–South Boundary Trail routes, see Route II.

36 For a description of this trail, see Route II, on page 52.

ROUTE II

1 Don Beers, *Jasper-Robson, A Taste of Heaven: Scenes, Tales, Trails* (Calgary, Highline, 1996), 40.

2 Aphrodite Karamitsanis, *Place Names of Alberta, Volume 1: Mountains, Mountain Parks and Foothills* (Calgary: University of Calgary Press, 1991), 41 and 123–24.

3 James G. MacGregor, *Overland by the Yellowhead* (Saskatoon: Western Producer Prairie Books, 1974), 130.

4 M.P. Bridgland and R. Douglas, *Description and Guide for Jasper Park* (Ottawa: Department of the Interior, 1917), 66.

5 J.N. Wallace, "Southesk's Journey through the West in 1859," J.N. Wallace Collection, Peel Special Collections Library, University of Alberta.

6 James Carnegie, Earl of Southesk, *Saskatchewan and the Rocky Mountains* (Rutland, VT: Charles E. Tuttle, 1969), 180.

7 Ibid, 201.

8 Ibid, 202.

9 Ibid, 1.

10 Ibid, 216–17.

11 Ibid, 225.

12 Ibid, 228.

13 Ibid, 229.

14 Ibid, 230.

15 Ibid.

16 For more information about this part of the trip, see *Life of the Trail 1: Historic Hikes in Eastern Banff National Park* (Calgary: Rocky Mountain Books, 2008), 73, 77.

17 For a description of this portion of the trip, see *Life of the Trail 3: The Historic Route from Old Bow Fort to Jasper* (Calgary: Rocky Mountain Books, 2009), 50.

18 A.P. Coleman, *The Canadian Rockies New & Old Trails* (Calgary: Aquila Books, 1999), 163–64.

19 For more information about this portion of the trip, see *Life of the Trail 1*, 170–73.

20 For more information about this route, see Route III, on page 121.

21 For more information about this trip, see Route I, on page 36.

22 Lillian Gest fonds, Whyte Museum of the Canadian Rockies, M67/41, 36–37.

23 For information about the Pipestone Pass trip, see *Life of the Trail 1*, 111–12.

24 Lillian Gest fonds, M67/41, 62–74.

25 For details of this portion of the trip, see *Life of the Trail 1*, 54–56.

26 For this portion of the trip, see *Life of the Trail 1*, 172.

27 Cyndi Smith, *Off the Beaten Track: Women Adventurers and Mountaineers in Western Canada* (Lake Louise: Coyote Books, 1989), 258, 264. Mona's sister, Agnes, was licensed at the same time. For more information about the Harragin sisters, see Route III, on page 115.

28 McDonald's headquarters cabin was on the Medicine Tent River; for shelter on the remainder of his route along the Brazeau River to Nigel Pass he built split log tepees chinked with moss. The remains of some of his tepees still existed many years later.

29 Frank Camp, *Roots in the Rockies* (Ucluelet: Frank Camp Enterprises, 1993), 23–24.

30 R.J. Burns with M. Schintz, *Guardians of the Wild: A History of the Warden Service of Canada's National Parks* (Calgary: University of Calgary Press, 2000), 188.

ROUTE III

1 For a description of this trip, see *Life of the Trail 3: The Historic Route from Old Bow Fort to Jasper* (Calgary: Rocky Mountain Books, 2009), 90.

2 R.W. Sandford, *Yoho: A History and Celebration of Yoho National Park* (Canmore: Altitude, 1993), 46.

3 Klyne's name has been variously spelled Klyne, Clyne, Kline, Cline and Klein. Today, only the spellings Klyne (referring to the man) and Cline (given to the geological features) are in use.

4 See sections below, McLeod's Maligne River Section, starting on page 112 and Coleman's Cline River, Cataract and Jonas Passes Section, starting on page 121 for details of these trips.

5 Lewis R. Freeman, *On the Roof of the Rockies* (Toronto: McClelland and Stewart, 1925), 13.

6 For details of this portion of the trip, see *Life of the Trail 3*, 174.

7 Fred Brewster, letter to Bruce H. Boreham, September 23, 1941, Major Fredrick Archibald Brewster fonds, (84.167.01.2.1) Jasper Yellowhead Museum and Archives.

8 For a description of this trail, see *Life of the Trail 2: Historic Hikes in Northern Yoho National Park* (Calgary: Rocky Mountain Books, 2008), 172-173.

9 E.J. Hart. *Jimmy Simpson: Legend of the Rockies* (Canmore: Altitude, 1991), 142.

10 See Route II, on page 69, above for details of this portion of the trip.

11 E.J. Hart, ed., *A Hunter of Peace: Mary T. S. Schäffer's Old Indian Trails of the Canadian Rockies* (Banff: the Whyte Foundation, 1980), 14.

12 James G. MacGregor, *Overland by the Yellowhead* (Saskatoon: Western Producer Prairie Books, 1974), 113.

13 For more details of this trip, see page 132.

14 See Route I, on page 33, for more details of this portion of the trip.

15 Brewster, letter to Bruce H. Boreham, 1941.

16 For more detail about these trips, see Route IV, on page 168.

17 Cyndi Smith, *Off the Beaten Track: Women Adventurers and Mountaineers in Western Canada* (Lake Louise: Coyote Books, 1989), 258.

18 Ibid, 267.

19 E.J. Hart, *Diamond Hitch: The Early Outfitters and Guides of Banff and Jasper* (Banff: Summerthought, 1979), 143.

20 For more information about the Nigel Pass trail, see page 126.

21 For more information about this portion of the trip, see *Life of the Trail 2*, 172.

22 Robson family fonds, Jasper Yellowhead Museum and Archives, 993.37.5.

23 See pages 132–35 for more information about the Maligne Pass route.

24 William C. Taylor, *Tracks Across my Trail: Donald "Curly" Phillips, Guide and Outfitter* (Jasper: Jasper–Yellowhead Society, 1984), 103–105.

25 A.Y. Jackson, *A Painter's Country: The Autobiography of A. Y. Jackson* (Toronto: Clarke Irwin and Company, 1958), 106–107.

26 Lisa Christensen, *A Hiker's Guide to Art of the Canadian Rockies* (Calgary: Glenbow Museum, 1996), 113.

27 Jackson, 106.

28 Ibid, 107.

29 For more information on this route, see pages 160–64.

30 A.P. Coleman, *The Canadian Rockies New & Old Trails* (Calgary: Aquila Books, 1999), 139–44.

31 For more information about this portion of the trip, see Route I, on page 30.

32 See Route II on page 65 for further details about this portion of the trip.

33 See Route I on page 31 for more information about this portion of the trip.

34 For information about this route, see *Life of the Trail 1: Historic Hikes in Eastern Banff National Park* (Calgary: Rocky Mountain Books, 2008), 168–73.

35 Coleman, 183.

36 Ibid, 181.

37 Ibid, 182.

38 Ibid, 209–10.

39 Ibid, 183–84.

40 Ibid, 185–86.

41 Don Beers, *Jasper–Robson, A Taste of Heaven: Scenes, Tales, Trails* (Calgary, Highline, 1996), 148.

42 Coleman, 233.

43 Beers, 153.

44 For a description of this trip, see *Life of the Trail 3*, 112.

45 Lillian Gest fonds, Whyte Museum of the Canadian Rockies, M67/41, 28–30.

46 See page 132 for a description of this trip.

47 See Route I on page 34 for a description of this trip.

48 Stanley Washburn, *Trails, Trappers and Tenderfeet in the New Empire Western Canada* (London: A. Melrose, 1912), 123–25.

49 Ibid, 148–56. See also Hart, 1979, 85. Hart indicates that it was Jonas Pass that was blocked by a landslide. Washburn's book does not specify which pass they crossed, but Jonas Pass would be out of their way; the connector to Poboktan Creek over Jonas Shoulder was not known until 1914; and the landslide was encountered after the party had crossed a pass. Moreover, it would have been a short trip back from Jonas Pass to Nigel Pass, but Washburn complains of a long trip back to the Brazeau and on to Nigel Pass. It seems most likely that it was Poboktan Pass they crossed, and the landslide was along Poboktan Creek, after they crossed the pass.

50 See Route I for a description of this area.

51 Hart, 1991, 71.

52 Ibid, 74.

53 Joseph McAleenan, "Hunting with Rifle and Camera in the Canadian Rockies" (1916), Whyte Museum of the Canadian Rockies, 04.2 MIIh, 6.

54 Hart, 1991, 77.

55 *Bighorn Wildland* (Calgary: Alberta Wilderness Association, 2003), 136.

56 See Route I for details on McGillivray's route.

57 Mary T.S. Schäffer, "Old Indian Trails: Expedition of 1907," In E.J. Hart, ed., 1980, 73.

58 See Route I on pages 33–34 for details of this route.

59 Mary T.S. Schäffer, "Old Indian Trails: Expedition of 1908," Quoted in E.J. Hart, ed., 1980, 91–92.

60 Ibid, 92.

61 Ibid.

62 Ibid.

63 Ibid, 93.

64 Ibid, 94.

65 Quoted E.J. Hart, ed., 1980, 14.

66 Smith, 87.

67 Taylor, 38.

68 Ibid, 39–40.

69 Donald Philllips, "Fitzhugh to Laggan," *Canadian Alpine Journal* 4 (1912), 88.

70 Taylor, 40–41.

71 Ibid, 41.

72 For descriptions of these trips, see pages 36, 69, 110, 119.

73 Beers, 144.

Route IV

1 The exact location of Buffalo Prairie (Prairie de la Vache) is unclear but the name may refer to the series of north–south meadows along the route.

2 Mary T.S. Schäffer, "The 1911 Expedition to Maligne Lake," In E.J. Hart, ed., *A Hunter of Peace: Mary T.S. Schäffer's Old Indian Trails of the Canadian Rockies* (Banff: the Whyte Foundation, 1980), 138.

3 Ibid, 139.

4 Ibid, 143.

5 Ibid.

6 Ibid, 144.

7 William C. Taylor, *Tracks Across my Trail: Donald "Curly" Phillips, Guide and Outfitter* (Jasper: Jasper–Yellowhead Society, 1984), 36–38.

8 Arthur O. Wheeler, "The Alpine Club of Canada's Expedition to Jasper Park, Yellowhead Pass and Mount Robson Region, 1911," *Canadian Alpine Journal* 4 (1912): 70.

9 Lawrence J. Burpee, *Among the Canadian Alps* (Toronto: Bell and Cockburn, 1914), 188.

10 Ibid, 182.

11 See page 120 for details of the first part of this trip.

12 A.Y. Jackson, *A Painter's Country: The Autobiography of A. Y. Jackson* (Toronto: Clarke Irwin and Company, 1958), 107.

13 "With the Trail Riders at Maligne," *Canadian National Railways Magazine* (September 1926), 15, 43.

14 See page 114 for details of this tour.

15 I.S. MacLaren, *Mapper of Mountains: M. P. Bridgland in the Canadian Rockies, 1902–1930* (Edmonton: University of Alberta Press, 2005), 115–18.

16 Cyndi Smith, *Jasper Park Lodge: In the Heart of the Canadian Rockies* (Canmore: Coyote Books, 1985), 55.

IMAGE CREDITS

Page 22 David Thompson is best known as a geographer, surveyor and map maker. This is an artist's depiction of what he looked like while surveying. (Courtesy Algonquin Park Visitor Center)

Page 28 Lucius Coleman, a rancher from Morley, accompanied his brother on all of his overland trips. He is shown here with other founding members of the Alpine Club of Canada, on the far right in the second row. (Whyte Museum of the Canadian Rockies, v14 ACOP-369)

Page 33 After the death of her first husband, Mary Schäffer learned to camp and ride so that she could explore the Rocky Mountains between Lake Louise and Jasper. (Whyte Museum of the Canadian Rockies, v527/PS-151)

Page 36 Lillian Gest spent 63 consecutive summers in the Canadian Rockies, often accompanying her friend, Caroline Hinman, on her Off the Beaten Track tours and hunting trips. (Whyte Museum of the Canadian Rockies, v225/PD-6, p-41)

Page 39 Caroline Hinman toured extensively throughout the Canadian Rockies, leading her Off the Beaten Track tours for young American girls. Outfitter Jim Boyce nicknamed her "Timberline Kate" because of her penchant for choosing campsites high on mountain sides or on a pass, in order to enjoy a good view. (Whyte Museum of the Canadian Rockies, v282/PD 10, p 10)

Page 41 Warden Charlie Matheson (r), shown here with outfitter Curly Phillips and Charlie's wife, Mona (nee Harragin). Matheson patrolled the backcountry in the Brazeau Lake region for many years. After their marriage, Mona joined in his pursuits. (Jasper–Yellowhead Museum and Archives 001.14.01.02.01)

Page 53 J.J. McArthur, a surveyor with the Topographic Survey of Canada, surveyed part of Southesk's route in 1884. The task required scaling many mountains with his partner, W.S. Drewry (above). (Library and Archives Canada, PA-023141)

Page 56 James Carnegie, Earl of Southesk, came to Canada on a pleasure trip to regain his health and to partake in the "sport" of shooting wild animals. His arsenal of fine weapons was put to good use on the trail, often shooting more animals than his party could use for food, leaving the carcasses for predators. (Glenbow Museum and Archives, NA-1355-1)

Page 68 Professor A.P. Coleman, one of the greatest explorers in the Canadian Rockies, used Stoney guide Jimmy Jacob's twentieth-century route along the Cline River and over Cataract Pass several times.

(Whyte Museum of the Canadian Rockies, v14/AC OOP-82)

Page 72 Caroline Hinman and Lillian Gest often rounded out their summer season of travels through the Rockies by taking a hunting trip with friends. This group consisted of (l–r) Polly Prescott, Lillian Gest, Margurite Schneffbacher and Caroline Hinman. (Whyte Museum of the Canadian Rockies v282/PD-10)

Page 73 Mona Harragin and her sister, Agnes, were the first female licensed guides in the Canadian National Parks. Mona, shown here loading a pack horse, was widely respected as a tough and independent guide. (Glenbow Museum and Archives, NA-2677-1)

Page 74 Telephones such as these were used widely in backcountry warden cabins in the 1930s. Injured Warden Ed McDonald knocked the receiver off the hook but had difficulty reaching the crank to activate the phone. (Jasper–Yellowhead Museum and Archives, 994.17.09)

Page 74 This improvised stretcher strung between two horses was used to carry injured warden Ed McDonald back to civilization. (l–r) Alex Wiley, guide Bruce Otto, unknown, Warden Matheson, and unknown. One of the unknown men (likely the one on the right) is Dr. Ross. The other may be Warden Frank Wells. (Jasper–Yellowhead Museum and Archives, 994.56.1605)

Page 75 Warden Ed McDonald recovering in hospital after the ordeal of breaking his pelvis while on patrol near the Rocky River. (Jasper–Yellowhead Museum and Archives, PA 98-312)

Page 106 Byron Harmon is the most celebrated photographer of the Canadian Rockies. In 1924 he and his friend, Lewis Freeman, completed a trip from Lake Louise to Jasper and back so Harmon could add to his extensive collection of mountain photographs. The last part of the route was along Old Klyne's Trail. (Whyte Museum of the Canadian Rockies, v263/NA-2400)

Page 108 Lewis Freeman accompanied his friend Byron Harmon on a trip from Lake Louise to Jasper and back. Freeman was a travel writer and took the opportunity to collect material for his book, On the Roof of the Rockies. (Whyte Museum of the Canadian Rockies, v263/NA-2242)

Page 113 Outfitter Fred Brewster, who had established his business in Fitzhugh (Jasper) in 1912, was awarded the contract to cut a trail up the Maligne River as far as Medicine Lake in 1914. This photo shows him lighting his pipe with a burning stick from a campfire. (Jasper–Yellowhead Museum and Archives, PA 7-52)

Page 117 (l–r) Charlie Matheson, Gwen Pickford, Charles Golden, Agnes Harragin and Mona Harragin. The Harragin sisters were the first licensed female guides in the national parks. The sisters later married local men and spent their lives in the Jasper–Hinton area. (Jasper–Yellowhead Museum and Archives, 990.01.12)

Page 119 Joan Robson, a long-time resident of Hinton, Alberta, participated in the 1927 Glacier Trail trip. (Jasper–Yellowhead Museum and Archives, 993.37.129)

Page 119 Jack Brewster, who initiated the Glacier Trail pack-train trips from Jasper to Lake Louise, is seen here on his July 1927 trip. (Jasper–Yellowhead Museum and Archives, 993-37-18-9)

Page 120 Artist A.Y. Jackson, who painted in the Rockies in the 1920s, returned to teach at the Banff School of Fine Arts. He is shown here (centre, front row) with the staff of the school, ca. 1940. (Glenbow Museum and Archives, NA-5660-15)

Page 129 Wildlife artist Carl Rungius first came to the Canadian Rockies at the invitation of Jimmy Simpson. He became so enamoured with the scenery and wildlife that he eventually bought a seasonal home in Banff. (Glenbow Museum and Archives, NA-3466-55)

Page 131 The Riviere family travelled with the Kopases on the last leg of their journey to Jasper, adding a light-hearted air to evening camps. In this playful camp scene, George Riviere is pretending to be a horse, with his wife, Maggie, and her sister, Annie, as riders. Ruth Kopas (in the white skirt) and the two men, Ray and Slim, enjoy the frolics. (Courtesy Keith Cole)

Page 133 Having been to Maligne Lake as a child of 14, Stoney Sampson Beaver drew Mary Schäffer a rough map of the route from memory. Schäffer had met the Beaver family on an earlier visit to the Kootenay Plains. (Whyte Museum of the Canadian Rockies, v527-v-53)

Page 158 Mary Schäffer was the first non-Native woman to travel extensively in the Rocky Mountains. It was her party that rediscovered Maligne Lake from the south in 1908. The federal government asked her to survey the lake in 1911, and she was instrumental in having the area retained within Jasper National Park. (Whyte Museum of the Canadian Rockies, v527 PD-1)

Page 161 The purpose of Mary Schäffer's 1911 trip to Maligne Lake was to survey the lake. Jonas was the unlucky horse relegated to carry the unwieldy planks

(16 feet long, 18 inches wide, and over an inch thick) required to construct a boat. The fact that it was no easy task was highlighted when he tripped during a stream crossing, embedding the boards in the far bank and pinning his head underwater. (Whyte Museum of the Canadian Rockies, v527/PS-131)

Page 163 Shovels, carved from a convenient tree, were used to clear snow from the top of the pass. From a distance, Mary Schäffer and companions mistook them for sheep. (Whyte Museum of the Canadian Rockies, v527/PS129)

Page 165 (l–r) Arthur Wheeler, Curly Phillips, Harry Blagden, J.H. Riley, Charles Walcott Jr., Reverend George Kinney (seated), James Shand-Harvey and Casey Jones were members of the 1911 ACC–Smithsonian party that explored in the Mount Robson and Maligne Lake areas. (Whyte Museum of the Canadian Rockies, V263 NA-5999.)

Page 167 Lawren Harris, one of the best known of the artists of the Group of Seven, was a war artist between 1914 and 1918. He is seen here in army uniform with his paint box. His trips to the Rockies began less than a decade later. (Library and Archives Canada, PA-116593)

All other photographs: Emerson Sanford

BIBLIOGRAPHY

Bighorn Wildland. Calgary: Alberta Wilderness Association, 2003.

Beers, Don. *Jasper-Robson, A Taste of Heaven: Scenes, Tales, Trails.* Calgary: Highline Publishing, 1996.

Bridgland, M.P. and R. Douglas. *Description of and Guide to Jasper Park.* Ottawa: Department of the Interior, 1917.

Burns, R.J. with M. Schintz. *Guardians of the Wild: A History of the Warden Service of Canada's National Parks.* Calgary: University of Calgary Press, 2000.

Burpee, Lawrence J. *Among the Canadian Alps.* Toronto: Bell and Cockburn, 1914.

Camp, Frank. *Roots in the Rockies.* Ucluelet: Frank Camp Enterprises, 1993.

Christensen, Lisa. *A Hiker's Guide to Art of the Canadian Rockies.* Calgary: Glenbow Museum, 1996.

Coleman, A.P. *The Canadian Rockies: New & Old Trails.* Calgary: Aquila Books, 1999.

Freeman, Lewis R. *On the Roof of the Rockies.* Toronto: McClelland and Stewart, 1925.

Hart, E.J. *Diamond Hitch: The Early Outfitters and Guides of Banff and Jasper.* Banff: Summerthought, 1979.

Hart, E.J., ed. *A Hunter of Peace, Mary T. S. Schäffer's Old Indian Trails of the Canadian Rockies.* Banff: The Whyte Foundation, 1980.

Hart, E.J. *Jimmy Simpson: Legend of the Rockies.* Canmore: Altitude, 1991.

Jackson, A.Y. *A Painter's Country: The Autobiography of A. Y. Jackson.* Toronto: Clarke Irwin and Company, 1958.

Karamitsanis, Aphrodite. *Place Names of Alberta, Volume I: Mountains, Mountain Parks and Foothills.* Calgary: University of Calgary Press, 1991.

Kopas, Cliff. *Packhorses to the Pacific: A Wilderness Honeymoon.* Victoria: TouchWood Editions, 2004.

Lillian Gest fonds. Whyte Museum of the Canadian Rockies. Banff, Alberta. M67.

MacGregor, James G. *Overland by the Yellowhead.* Saskatoon: Western Producer Prairie Books, 1974.

MacLaren, I.S. *Mapper of Mountains: M. P. Bridgland in the Canadian Rockies 1902–1930.* Edmonton: University of Alberta Press, 2005.

Major Frederick Archibald Brewster fonds. Jasper–Yellowhead Museum and Archives. Jasper, Alberta.

McAleenan, Joseph. "Hunting with Rifle and Camera in the Canadian Rockies" (1916). Whyte Museum of the Canadian Rockies. Banff, Alberta. 04.2 M1 1h.

McCart, Joyce and Peter. *On the Road with David Thompson.* Calgary: Fifth House, 2000.

Morton, Arthur S. "The Last of Fort George and Duncan M'Gillivray." In *The Journal of Duncan M'Gillivray of the North West Company at Fort George on the Saskatchewan, 1794–5, With Introduction, Notes and Appendix by Arthur S. Morton* (Toronto: Macmillan, 1929).

Phillips, Donald. "Fitzhugh to Laggan." *Canadian Alpine Journal* 4 (1912): 87–91.

Robson family fonds. Jasper Yellowhead Museum and Archives. Jasper, Alberta. 993.37.5.

Sandford, R.W. *Yoho: A History and Celebration of Yoho National Park.* Canmore: Altitude, 1993.

Sanford Beck, Janice. *No Ordinary Woman: The Story of Mary Schäffer Warren.* Calgary: Rocky Mountain Books, 2001.

Schäffer, Mary T.S. "Old Indian Trails: Expedition of 1907." In E.J. Hart, ed. *A Hunter of Peace: Mary T. S. Schäffer's Old Indian Trails of the Canadian Rockies.* Banff: The Whyte Foundation, 1980.

Schäffer, Mary T.S. "Old Indian Trails: Expedition of 1908." In E.J. Hart, ed. *A Hunter of Peace: Mary T. S. Schäffer's Old Indian Trails of the Canadian Rockies.* Banff: The Whyte Foundation, 1980.

Schäffer, Mary T. S. "The 1911 Expedition to Maligne Lake." In E.J. Hart, ed. *A Hunter of Peace: Mary T. S. Schäffer's Old Indian Trails of the Canadian Rockies.* Banff: The Whyte Foundation, 1980.

Smith, Cyndi. *Jasper Park Lodge: In the Heart of the Canadian Rockies.* Canmore: Coyote Books, 1985.

Smith, Cyndi. *Off the Beaten Track: Women Adventurers and Mountaineers in Western Canada.* Lake Louise: Coyote Books, 1989.

Southesk, James Carnegie, Earl of. *Saskatchewan and the Rocky Mountains*. Rutland, VT: Charles E. Tuttle, 1969.

Taylor, William C. *Tracks Across my Trail: Donald "Curly" Phillips, Guide and Outfitter*. Jasper: Jasper–Yellowhead Historical Society, 1984.

Wallace, J.N. "Southesk's Journey through the West in 1859." J.N. Wallace Collection. Peel Special Collections Library. University of Alberta.

Wheeler, Arthur O. "The Alpine Club of Canada's Expedition to Jasper Park, Yellowhead Pass and Mount Robson Region, 1911." *Canadian Alpine Journal* 4 (1912): 1–83.

"With the Trail Riders at Maligne." *Canadian National Railways Magazine* (September 1926): 15, 43.

INDEX

About the Authors

EMERSON SANFORD, originally from Nova Scotia, first visited the mountains of western Canada in the summer of 1961. Eleven years later, he moved to Alberta and has been hiking ever since. After beginning to backpack seriously with his teenaged daughters in 1990, he began to wonder who cut the trails and how their routing had been determined. Since then, not only has he delved through printed material about the trails, he has also solo hiked every historic route and most long trails between Mount Robson and the Kananaskis Lakes – over 3000 kilometres over five years! Emerson now lives in Canmore with his wife, Cheryl.

JANICE SANFORD BECK is the author of the best-selling *No Ordinary Woman: the Story of Mary Schäffer Warren* (Rocky Mountain Books, 2001). She has also written the introduction to the latest edition of Mary T.S. Schäffer's *Old Indian Trails of the Canadian Rockies* (Rocky Mountain Books, 2007) and, with Cheryl Sanford, researched the Mary Schäffer Warren portion of the Glenbow Museum's new permanent exhibit, *Mavericks*. Janice is presently masquerading as a flatlander, making her home in Saskatoon with her partner, Shawn, and their three children.

FURTHER READING ...

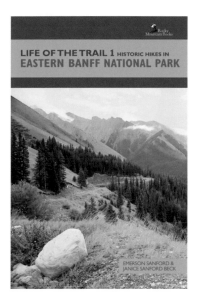

LIFE OF THE TRAIL I

Historic Hikes in Eastern Banff National Park

Emerson Sanford & Janice Sanford Beck

Life of the Trail 1: Historic Hikes in Eastern Banff National Park follows the trails of David Thompson, Walter Wilcox, the Palliser Expedition, James Carnegie Earl of Southesk, Bill Peyto and A.P. Coleman. Along the way, the reader will journey from the Kootenay Plains to Lake Minnewanka, discovering the stories behind routes through the mountain towns of Banff and Lake Louise and along the Red Deer, Ptarmigan and Skoki valleys.

ISBN 978-1-894765-99-2

Colour and Black & White Photos, Maps

$26.95, Softcover

LIFE OF THE TRAIL 2

Historic Hikes in Northern Yoho National Park

Emerson Sanford & Janice Sanford Beck

Life of the Trail 2: Historic Hikes in Northern Yoho National Park follows the trails of fur traders La Gasse and Le Blanc, the Palliser Expedition, Tom Wilson, J.J. McArthur, Professor Jean Habel, Walter Wilcox, C.S. Thompson, David Thompson, Jimmy Simpson and Jack Brewster. Along the way, the reader will journey past pristine lakes and glaciers that have become legendary throughout the world, discovering the stories behind routes through the mountain towns of Lake Louise and Field; over Howse, Amiskwi, Bow and Burgess passes; and along Yoho, Emerald and Castleguard rivers.

ISBN 978-1-897522-00-4

Colour and Black & White Photos, Maps

$26.95, Softcover

Life of the Trail 3

Historic Trails from Old Bow Fort to Jasper

Emerson Sanford & Janice Sanford Beck

Life of the Trail 3: The Historic Route from Old Bow Fort to Jasper starts at the remains of Peigan Post, originally built in 1832 and still visible today, located at the west end of the Morley Reserve. This entire route is now a contemporary road, but early in the 20th century the section north of Lake Louise was the main trail heading north and was very busy with pioneers, adventurers and explorers. The trail has been divided into three sections: Old Bow Fort to Lake Louise, Lake Louise to Sunwapta Pass and Sunwapta Pass to Jasper.

ISBN 978-1-897522-41-7

Colour and Black & White Photos, Maps

$26.95, Softcover

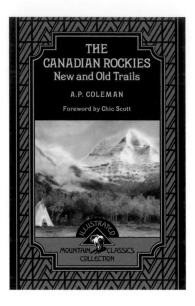

THE CANADIAN ROCKIES: NEW AND OLD TRAILS
Mountain Classics Collection 1

A.P. Coleman
Foreword by Chic Scott

First published in 1911, this book gives modern-day readers a glimpse of the early days of mountaineering in the Canadian West. It paints a sympathetic picture of the rugged men and women who opened the region and of the hardships they endured.

ISBN 978-1-897522-50-9
Black & White Photos
$19.95, Softcover

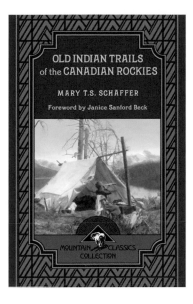

OLD INDIAN TRAILS OF THE CANADIAN ROCKIES
Mountain Classics Collection 2

Mary T.S. Schäffer
Foreword by Janice Sanford Beck

Mary T.S. Schäffer was an avid explorer and one of the first non-Native women to venture into the heart of the Canadian Rocky Mountains, where few women – or men – had gone before. First published in 1911, *Old Indian Trails of the Canadian Rockies* is Schäffer's story of her adventures in the traditionally male-dominated world of climbing and exploration.

ISBN 978-1-897522-49-3
Black & White Photos
$19.95 Softcover

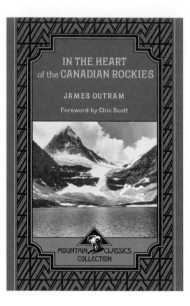

IN THE HEART OF THE CANADIAN ROCKIES

Mountain Classics Collection 3

James Outram
Foreword by Chic Scott

Born in 1864 in London, England, James Outram was a Church of England clergyman, mountaineer, author, businessman, militia officer and Orangeman who came to Canada at the turn of the 20th century after travelling and climbing throughout Europe. First published in 1905, *In the Heart of the Canadian Rockies* is Outram's record of his adventures and exploits in the early years of the 20th century among the massive mountains straddling the Alberta–British Columbia boundary.

ISBN 978-1-894765-96-1
$22.95, Softcover

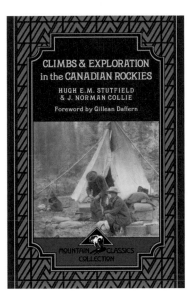

CLIMBS & EXPLORATION IN THE CANADIAN ROCKIES
Mountain Classics Collection 4

Hugh E.M. Stutfield & J. Norman Collie
Foreword by Gillean Daffern

First published in 1903, *Climbs & Exploration in the Canadian Rockies* details the mountaineering adventures of Hugh Stutfield and J. Norman Collie while the two were together during various explorations in the area north of Lake Louise, Alberta. Between 1898 and 1902, Stutfield and Collie journeyed through the mountain towns, valleys and passes of the Rockies, where Collie completed numerous first ascents and discovered fresh views of Lake Louise and the Columbia Icefield.

ISBN 978-1-897522-06-6
$22.95, Softcover

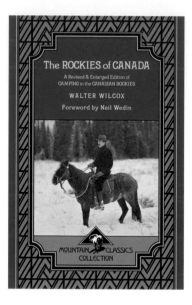

THE ROCKIES OF CANADA
Mountain Classics Collection 5

Walter Wilcox
Foreword by Neil Wedin

First published in 1900, *The Rockies of Canada* is based on one of the first major works to be written about the mountains of western Canada, *Camping in the Canadian Rockies* (1896). Focusing on the escapades and first ascents of the "Lake Louise Club," a group of relatively inexperienced climbers from Yale University and elsewhere in the eastern United States, this book offers the reader a glimpse not only of the remarkable beauty and grandeur of Banff, Lake Louise and the Rocky Mountains, but also the danger and rigours these early adventurers experienced nearly every day.

ISBN 978-1-897522-14-1
$19.95, Softcover

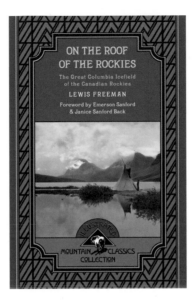

ON THE ROOF OF THE ROCKIES

Mountain Classics Collection 6

Lewis Ransome Freeman
Foreword by Emerson Sanford and Janice Sanford Beck

This book details the amazing efforts undertaken by Lewis Freeman and Byron Harmon to scientifically explore and comprehensively photograph during their 70-day, 500-mile journey through the Canadian Rockies and Columbia Mountains. With a guide, a wrangler, a cook, 16 horses, two dogs, some carrier pigeons and hundreds of pounds of what was then state-of-the-art photography, moviemaking and radio equipment, the group journeyed through the area contemplating the routes of earlier explorers, facing violent storms and ultimately preserving historic views of pristine wilderness for future generations.

ISBN 978-1-897522-46-2
Black & White Photos
$19.95, Softcover

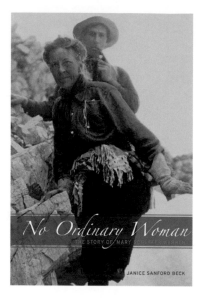

No Ordinary Woman

The Story of Mary Schäffer Warren

Janice Sanford Beck

Artist, photographer, writer, world traveller and, above all, explorer, Mary Schäffer Warren overcame the limited expectations of women at the turn of the 19th century in order to follow her dreams.

ISBN 978-0-921102-82-3
Colour and Black & White Photos
$24.95, Softcover

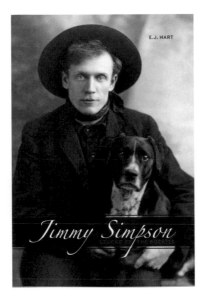

JIMMY SIMPSON
Legend of the Rockies

E.J. Hart

The Stoney Indians called him "Nashan-esen" meaning "wolverine-go-quick" because of his speed in travelling on snowshoes over the rugged landscape of the Candian Rockies. This book is the story of Jimmy Simpson's 80-year epic as one of the most important guides, outfitters, lodge operators, hunters, naturalists and artists in the Canadian Rockies.

ISBN 978-1-897522-25-7

Black & White Photos

$24.95, Softcover

50 Roadside Panoramas

In the Canadian Rockies

Dave Birrell

Dave Birrell brings you 50 panoramas taken from highway viewpoints in the Canadian Rockies and the Eastern Slopes between Yellowhead Pass and Waterton. Photographs are accompanied by knowledgeable text, providing you with the fascinating stories behind the names of geographical features: mountains, passes, valleys and lakes.

ISBN 978-0921102-65-6
Black & White Photos, Maps
$24.95, Softcover

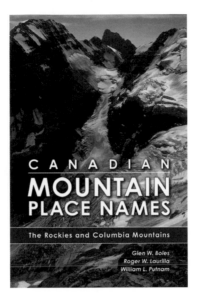

CANADIAN MOUNTAIN PLACE NAMES
The Rockies and Columbia Mountains

Glen W. Boles, Roger W. Laurilla, William L. Putnam

This is an entertaining and informative treatise on the toponymy of this increasingly popular alpine region, featuring the names of peaks, rivers, lakes and other geographic landmarks.

ISBN 978-1-894765-79-4
Black & White Photos, Line Drawings
$19.95, Softcover

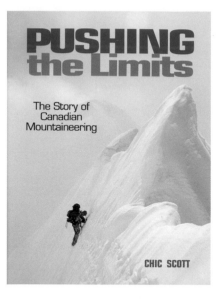

PUSHING THE LIMITS
The Story of Canadian Mountaineering

Chic Scott

Journeying to the summits, the crags and the gyms, from the West Coast to Québec and from the Yukon to the Rockies, Chic introduces his readers to early mountain pioneers and modern-day climbing athletes.

ISBN 978-0921102-59-5
Colour and Black & White Photos, Prints, Maps
$59.95, Hardcover

ACKNOWLEDGEMENTS

The preparation for a book of this type requires the perusal of many secondary sources; during our research we read hundreds of books. The authors of the books used are acknowledged in the Notes section at the end of this book. Many of the books are still in print and readily available. Others required much diligence on the part of reference librarians to obtain interlibrary loans, and we wish to thank the personnel at the Canmore Public Library, especially Michelle Preston and Hélène Lafontaine, for their assistance. Other books and documents were available only through the Whyte Museum and Archives, and we appreciate the efforts of Lena Goon, Elizabeth Kundert-Cameron, D.L. Cameron and Ted Hart for steering us on the right track and obtaining materials for us.

The Alpine Club of Canada in Canmore kindly allowed us the use of their collection of the *Canadian Alpine Journal*. Others who provided useful discussion and/or materials during the course of the research were: Carol at the Bruce Peel Special Collections Library at the University of Alberta, who was diligent in her search for the J.N. Wallace Manuscript Collection; Ron Tozer, Algonquin Park archivist; Lorna Dishkin of the BC Central Coast Archives; Keith Cole; Rene Morton; Thomas Peterson;

I.S. MacLaren; Meghan Power, Jasper-Yellowhead Museum and Archives; Melanie Gagnon, Library and Archives Canada; Kelly-Ann Turkington, Royal British Columbia Museum; Joyce Hildebrand, Alberta Wilderness Association; and Steve Waite, Glenbow Museum.

A large part of the effort in preparing these volumes was in hiking all of the trails and routes described in the history section. Emerson wishes to thank his wife, Cheryl, for the many hours she spent taking him to trailheads and picking him up several days later at a different location, sometimes on remote gravel roads that were not easily accessible. In addition, Cheryl always had in hand a copy of the itinerary for the hike in order to contact the Warden Service if the solo hiker did not emerge from the wilderness at the appointed time (he always did).

In addition, Emerson wishes to acknowledge the many hikers on remote backcountry trails who stopped to chat and made the solitary hikes more enjoyable. Many of these people are mentioned in the text. Others who are not mentioned met Emerson on trails near Lake Minnewanka, Athabasca Pass, Wildflower Creek valley, the Jasper Park North and South Boundary, Job Pass, the Rockwall and undoubtedly others. There were also several wardens along the way who contributed to the enjoyment of the backcountry experience.

For Janice, this project has been a labour of love, squeezed in amongst various family, community and work responsibilities. She would like to thank her partner, Shawn, and children, Robin, Rowan and Christopher, for their willingness to accommodate the time required for a project of this magnitude. She would also like to thank her parents for sharing their love of history and introducing her to the trails these volumes bring to life.

Finally, the authors would like to express their appreciation to Don Gorman, Meaghan Craven, Chyla Cardinal and others at Rocky Mountain Books for their efforts in bringing this work from manuscript to publication.